EARTH HEROES

Champions of the Ocean

By Fran Hodgkins
Illustrations by Cris Arbo

DAWN Publications

To my sisters, Barb and Beth, and my brother, Tom, with much love. — FH

To all my dear Virginia Beach friends. — CA

Copyright © 2009 Fran Hodgkins

Illustration copyright © 2009 Cris Arbo

A Sharing Nature With Children Book

All rights reserved.

Library of Congress Cataloging-in-Publication Data

Hodgkins, Fran, 1964-
   Earth heroes : champions of the ocean / by Fran Hodgkins ; illustrations by Cris Arbo. -- 1st ed.
     p. cm. -- (A sharing nature with children book)
     Summary: "The youth, career and lasting contributions of some of the world's greatest
naturalists and environmentalists are featured in this series of books on champions of the
wilderness, oceans, and wildlife, this volume focused on the oceans" – Provided by the publisher.
   Includes bibliographical references.
   ISBN 978-1-58469-119-8 (pbk.)
   1. Oceanographers--Biography--Juvenile literature. I. Arbo, Cris, ill. II. Title.
   GC30.A1H64 2009
   551.46092'2--dc22
   [B]

2009017926

Printed in U.S.A.

10 9 8 7 6 5 4 3 2 1

First Edition

Book design and computer production by Patty Arnold, *Menagerie Design and Publishing.*

Printed on recycled paper

DAWN PUBLICATIONS

12402 Bitney Springs Road
Nevada City, CA 95959
530-274-7775
nature@dawnpub.com

Mixed Sources
Product group from well-managed
forests and recycled wood or fiber
www.fsc.org Cert no. SCS-COC-00905
FSC © 1996 Forest Stewardship Council

TABLE OF CONTENTS

Beginning at the Beginning

Everything starts with an idea. That may sound obvious. But every great achievement in human history has started with one person having one idea.

"Hey, what would happen if we tamed those wolves and got them working with us?"

"You know, I think that horse could carry me if I got on it."

"Let's try using this fluffy plant fiber to make cloth, because animal hides make me itch."

Well, those probably aren't exact quotes! But you get the point: we domesticated the dog, learned to ride the horse, and started wearing cloth instead of skins—all because someone thought of it, and then tried.

The human ability to *make* things is phenomenal. Just look around you at the evidence, including this book (I happen to think that books are one of humanity's best-ideas-ever). But beyond making things is the idea that we humans inherited a magnificent planet, whose complexity and value we have just begun to understand. Over the years some key people have shared an important idea: that both understanding and protecting our planetary heritage is vital. And they've acted on that idea to make it a reality.

The companion book to this one, *Earth Heroes: Champions of the Wilderness*, profiles men and women who realized that the wild areas of our planet need protection. This book is about the men and women who have worked to help us understand the ocean and learn how to protect it. They have had a lot of ideas. This book is about those heroic people.

Sometimes ideas don't pan out as hoped. Jacques Cousteau's early attempt to make an underwater breathing device almost killed him.

Sometimes the ideas involve looking at something that already exists, but in a new way. Sylvia Earle looked at the Jim Suit, which was used to repair underwater oil platforms, and saw a kind of self-contained deep-diving one-person sub.

Ideas often involve asking *Why?* or *What if?* "What if sharks are not merely mindless killers?" asked Eugenie Clark. "What if people could hear the beautiful sounds humpback whales make?" asked Roger Payne. "Why do sea turtles disappear, and where do they go?" asked Archie Carr. Curiosity is key to coming up with ideas.

Sometimes we forget to be curious. We let the everyday stuff suck the joy of curiosity out of our lives. Or we listen to people who say that science is only for geeks.

Curiosity and science are for everybody: male and female, young and old.

Do you think scientists aren't athletic? Say that to the people in this book who have SCUBA-dived for literally thousands of hours or who have climbed to the tops of trees and the tops of mountains as they pursued an idea.

Do you think scientists aren't heroic? Say that to the people in this book who have stood firm for an idea, despite being vilified by colleagues and opponents. It's a hard and lonely thing to take a stand when everyone else thinks you're wrong.

Do you think scientists are dull people who don't have a life? Go online and listen to talks by Sylvia Earle and Tierney Thys. Curl up with the writing of William Beebe or Archie Carr. Listen to the whale songs that Roger Payne recorded.

Do you think science is just for people with degrees? More and more, researchers are turning to "citizen scientists"—people just like you and me—for help in their work. Tierney Thys, for example, has a page on her web site, www.oceansunfish.org, for citizen scientists to use and report encounters with the sea creatures she's been studying for more than a decade, the ocean sunfish.

As you read about these amazing people and their ideas, I hope that you'll have questions, questions that lead to ideas. Follow your questions and your ideas. You never know what might happen.

Earth Heroes: Champions of the Ocean

William Beebe

1877–1962

The First Celebrity Naturalist

"To be a Naturalist is better even than to be a King."

The sunlight streamed through the canopy of leaves far overhead, lighting the path the tall, lanky twelve-year-old boy followed into the woods. He walked as silently as he could, imitating his hero Uncas, from James Fenimore Cooper's novel *The Last of the Mohicans*. He loved the woods and was pleased that his footfalls did not disturb the activities of the birds and animals that surrounded him, seen and unseen, heard and silent.

Ahead he saw a chipmunk, a small ground squirrel, perched on a rock, facing away from him. Will forced himself to be even more quiet, drifting toward the skittish little creature like a mist. The chipmunk did not notice him at all; Will stood, unmoving, and watched as it groomed itself in the sun and surveyed the world with its bright black eyes.

Finally, the chipmunk turned its head a bit further around and caught a glimpse of Will. It leaped off the rock and dashed for cover. The boy relaxed. To have gotten so close to such a shy creature was a tremendous accomplishment for a young naturalist. He looked forward to telling his parents about it, and turned around to head back home.

Many children of the time enjoyed throwing rocks into ponds and watching polliwogs, but not William Beebe. Will took his interest in science and nature seriously, and he took very careful notes. He kept count of the species he saw and identified around his home in East Orange, New Jersey. He also collected specimens, shooting birds and small mammals and preserving their skins. His curiosity drove

William Beebe as a nine year old boy.

him to find out everything he possibly could about anything he encountered—animal, vegetable, or mineral.

Will's ability to observe and his willingness to take chances would make him one of America's great naturalists. In his fifties, he would become one of first people to see the great black depths of the deep ocean.

Charles William Beebe was born in Brooklyn on July 29, 1877, the son of a paper salesman and a former teacher. His parents encouraged their son's interest in science and nature. His father sent him bird and animal specimens he gathered on his business trips to upstate New York. At eight, he wrote in a letter to his father about how he had climbed a tree and taken several robin's eggs out of a nest. The boy put them in his mouth for safekeeping, but on the way down, young Will fell. "I swallered [the eggs,]" he reported sadly.

As a child, Will began keeping a journal and took copious notes about his observations, a practice he would keep up his whole life. Everything fascinated him. He made it his personal mission to find out everything possible about the creatures and plants he saw. Other neighborhood children brought eggs, insects, and animals for him to identify, which greatly pleased him. "I am beginning to be a Celebrated Naturalist," he wrote at age fourteen.

In his journals, Will made remarkably elaborate plans for his future. At the end of each year, he reviewed his accomplishments, and noted where he had fallen short of the goals he had set for himself at the year's beginning. For 1894, he wrote:

My expectations . . . are as follows:

In New Jersey, I expect to see at least 60 kinds of birds, 6 kinds of mammals, 6 kinds of reptiles, 6 kinds of fishes.

I expect to kill at least 100 animals and birds, say 25 varieties.

I expect to collect 100 insects (50 var.)

I expect to make notes on at least 250 days in the year.

I expect to see at least 4000 crows migrating.

At least 4000 crows? His mother, Henrietta, was a former teacher who had entertained Will and his friends by taking them on nature walks, and she instilled in him the ability to count crows. Will developed the ability to gauge the size of any flock or group of creatures—an important observational skill. Will studiously recorded his crow observations in his notebook.

After Will graduated from high school, his mother convinced two giants of natural history— paleontologist Henry Fairfield Osborne and ornithologist Frank Chapman—to oversee Will's scientific education. He entered Columbia University already knowing far more about nature than other students.

During college, Will traveled to Nova Scotia, Canada, where the ocean's vastness struck him for the first time. In a friend's boat he went out on the Bay of Fundy to learn how to dredge, or gather a sample of sea-bottom animals with a boxlike device dragged behind a boat. In his August 10, 1898, journal entry, Will

Will, at age eighteen, in his room surrounded by animal specimens.

wrote, "Dredging is the most fascinating work I have ever done. It keeps the excitement up to the highest pitch all the time, no one knowing what will come up in the next haul." It was the young naturalist's introduction to the amazing organisms that lived beneath the waves.

For the moment, though, the call of the ocean would have to wait; Will needed to make a living. His writings and photographs brought some income, but in 1899 he left Columbia without earning a degree. Instead he chose to pursue an exciting opportunity to be assistant curator for ornithology at the newly established New York Zoological Park.

On December 31, 1899, when he was twenty-two, he wrote,

> It is new for me in many ways—a new job; a new home; new opportunities; new friends; more money than I have ever had before, and yet I am not happy altogether. . . . I hope soon to spend each day more profitably and better. . . . What a day for new resolves to be made and kept.
>
> I have hundreds that cannot be written but although I will probably [go] back [on] them many times, I will keep them in the end. . . . I have spoken!

Earth Heroes: Champions of the Ocean

The declaration "I have spoken!" shows the young man's determination to make his words and thoughts become reality.

Will was living at a turning point in American science. During the 1800s and earlier, it was enough for a person to be a self-taught explorer of the natural world; formal scientific training wasn't required for a person to make contributions to the body of knowledge. In the 1900s, that began to change as colleges and universities formalized science education. Researchers began to need advanced degrees in a scientific specialty to be taken seriously. Despite his tremendous knowledge and scientific ability, Will would struggle to have others take him seriously because he lacked a degree.

Even though his work appeared in scholarly journals such as *Zoologica* and *Science*, this lack of academic credentials would eventually haunt him, especially because he loved to write books and articles that made science accessible, and even enjoyable, to the public. His articles in *The Atlantic Monthly*, *Boys and Girls Magazine*, and *The Ladies' Home Journal* were very popular. His friend and mentor Osborne quietly warned him that the popular writing he was doing could damage his scientific credibility. To be popular with lay people, it was believed, meant that a person was not a serious scientist. For many years after Beebe, other scientists (such as astronomer Carl Sagan) would encounter the same prejudice.

Will took the hint and devoted more time to scientific research, which pleased his boss at the zoo. Soon, Will received the opportunity for field study when he was named head of the zoo's new Department of Tropical Research, which would lead him to jungles and, eventually, to the deep ocean.

As part of his work, Will traveled to collect live animals for the zoo and preserved specimens and skins for the American Museum of Natural History. He journeyed to Java, Malaysia, Mexico, the Galapagos Islands, and Asia. He prepared an authoritative monograph on the world's pheasants. Nevertheless, despite Osborne's warning, he continued writing popular books and articles. His accounts of his adventures won him legions of fans, including President Theodore Roosevelt, cartoonist Rube Goldberg, and actors Douglas Fairbanks and Katherine Hepburn.

As he explored, he found himself increasingly drawn to the ocean. Using the clunky diving helmets that were the only equipment available at the time, he marveled at how cormorants and sea lions, so awkward on land, became swift and graceful in the water. Perhaps it would be possible to devise a vessel that would allow him to dive deeper and see what marvelous creatures lived there. He discussed his ideas with Roosevelt, and together they debated what kind of vessel would be best for deep-sea diving.

Fortunately, they were not the only people who were thinking about the issue. One day in 1929, an earnest young man named Otis Barton introduced himself through a mutual acquaintance. Barton had heard of Will's plan for a vessel that would allow him to explore the deep ocean. Barton thought that a sphere was the logical shape for such a vehicle to withstand the crushing pressure of the water at great depth.

Although we aren't aware of it, at the surface we are being pushed down upon by the atmosphere with a force of 14.7 pounds per square inch—an amount of pressure called, appropriately, one *atmosphere*. With every 33 feet we descend below the surface, we are under the pressure of an additional atmosphere. At 100 feet, nearly 60 pounds pushes down on every square inch of surface area. At 1000 feet, the pressure equals 30 atmospheres, or 445 pounds on every square inch!

Barton had already designed a vessel to withstand such extreme pressure, and he had a proposition: he would build the diving sphere if Will would dive with him. Will agreed.

Although Barton had designed the sphere, Will named it. He called it a "bathysphere" from the Greek word *bathus*, meaning "deep," and sphere. Another designer, a naval architect named John Butler, finalized the plans and hired the firms to build the sphere.

The list of firms he hired reads like a "Who's Who" of early 20th century industry. The Roebling company, designer and builder of the nation's first suspension bridge, supplied the 3,500-foot cable that would tie the bathysphere to the surface. Bell Laboratories, founded by telephone inventor Alexander Graham Bell, donated the equipment that would allow communication between the surface and the bathysphere. General Electric Company provided three windows made from pure quartz, each eight inches across and three inches thick, that withstood high pressure better than any glass window could. Atlas Foundry cast the steel ball and Watson-Stillman Hydraulics finished it. The first version of the bathysphere was completed in just six months.

But it weighed five tons. The winches available to lift it simply couldn't handle such a weight. So the bathysphere was melted down and redesigned. Weighing half the original, the second bathysphere was just

Will, left, and Otis Barton both squeezed themselves into the bathosphere, which was designed to protect them from the extreme pressures of the deep ocean.

four-and-a-half feet in diameter—a very tight fit for two occupants. The small hatch forced occupants to slide in and out, much like seals, Will noted. Once inside, one man sat while the other knelt, leaning back on his heels. The Bathysphere's cold, uninsulated metal hull chilled the men, adding to their discomfort.

The first dive took place off Bermuda on June 6, 1930. Both Will and Barton struggled to control their fear as the craft descended. At 300 feet, they discovered a leak. At 600 feet, a loose connection in the searchlight's electrical line set off sparks. At 700 feet, the bathysphere groaned unnervingly under the pressure. At 803 feet, even though he had made only few notes, Will decided to stop the descent and head back to the surface. Before he did, though, he marveled at the deep blue color surrounding them and said, "We are the first living men to look out at the strange illumination." That night, the team celebrated with dinner and dancing.

Six days later, they went even deeper, reaching 1,426 feet. What he saw through the glass windows startled him so much that the usually eloquent Will was often reduced to a series of "Oh's!" and "Ah's!" He described what he saw via the telephone system to Gloria Hollister, telling her about the bright explosions of light that appeared as brilliant as fireworks and faded just as fast; about the delicate jellyfish that glowed and pulsed as they swam; about the fish that made their own light. It was so astonishing that many people couldn't believe it.

In its June 1931 issue, *National Geographic* published Will's article about the dives. Barton, who realized that he couldn't afford to support the bathysphere anymore, donated it to Will and the New York Zoological

Society, asking that Will invite him should the bathysphere be used to dive again.

Weather and equipment issues prevented dives in 1931, and the bathysphere languished in storage. In 1932, Will succeeded in making more dives. This time, the media was along for the trip. A broadcast team from NBC radio joined Will, Barton, and the rest of the team in Bermuda. The plan was to do a live radio broadcast from the bathysphere while it was submerged. Not only would the NBC broadcast Will's words to the nation, but also the British Broadcasting Company would send them across England. Millions of people tuned in to hear the famous naturalist describe the amazing sights he saw:

> Miss Hollister ... tells me we are now at 1,550 feet...The color of the water is the bluest black imaginable. . . . At 1,700 feet, it is pitch dark inside and outside. . . . At 1,950 feet, the sea is boiling with lights and I can make out jet black comets. . . .We are at 2,000 feet. Five hatchet fish just passed, *Argyropelecus*, two or three inches long. The biggest fish yet just went by. It is shaped like a barracuda. The greenest light seen yet. I can actually get full outlines of fish. Loads of little—I don't know what they are.

Even though the dive at 2,200 feet was 440 feet short of the half-mile goal, the broadcast was a roaring success. Telegraphs poured in to congratulate Will, and newspapers all over the country carried the story. Yet in his year-end self-analysis, Will worried that the dives were really just publicity stunts, and that they were not advancing his reputation as a scientist.

As the Great Depression worsened, finding money to pay for expeditions became increasingly difficult. At last, Will hit on a new sponsor: the National Geographic Society. Founded in 1888, the society had the goal of supporting scientific research and spreading scientific knowledge. Its president, Gilbert Grosvenor, agreed to give Will a ten-thousand-dollar grant to support the dives of 1934. In exchange, Will would write two articles for the society's magazine about his experiences.

Being paid in advance was new for Will, and he wasn't comfortable with it. For all his other writing, he had been paid after he had finished. Nevertheless, he needed the Society's support. His first article, about the 1932 dive, wasn't very good, even by his own judgment, and the editor and he agreed to change the terms of the agreement: one long article instead of two short ones. Feeling better about the arrangement, Will moved ahead.

The bathysphere had been refitted since its earlier dives. An improved system for cleaning the air and removing carbon dioxide inside the sphere had been installed. Bell Telephone donated new telephone headsets; they wanted the original headsets for their company museum! And Barton brought along his camera, hoping to catch images of the deep sea's denizens that would make his Hollywood dreams come true.

The rest of Will's support team returned with him to Bermuda for the dives that would change history. After a few unmanned dives to make sure that the new equipment on the bathysphere functioned properly, Will chose August 11 for their first descent. On the way down, they saw dozens of fish, both familiar and strange. The oddest creatures hovered outside the bathysphere's windows at about 1,400 feet down: fish that were the color of "sickly sprouts of plants in the cellar" with oddly reduced tail fins and oversized vertical fins. He named the new specimen *Bathyembryx istiophasma*, "which is a Grecian way of saying that it comes from deep in the abyss and swims with ghost sails." They reached a depth of 2,510 feet before deciding enough was enough for one day. On the way back up, however, Will spotted another new fish through the bathysphere's window, which he called the three-starred anglerfish.

The naming of new species is not undertaken lightly, as you'll read more about in the chapter about Archie Carr. Usually a specimen that represents the species must be presented for taxonomists (scientists who classify living things) to study closely, comparing and contrasting it with

In the pitch blackness of the very deep sea, Will was astonished to see a world so full of bioluminescence—like the toothy anglerfish with its protruding luminous lure—that it resembled a sparkling night sky.

William Beebe

known specimens to determine if it truly is new to science. The specimen is key. Although Will was normally very cautious about naming new species, he thought he was justified in naming some of the animals he saw, due to the unusual circumstances and the unlikelihood of their ever being seen again.

However well intentioned his actions, Will caused a fury of controversy. Taxonomists argued that his naming of "new" species was irresponsible. Will was wounded by this reaction; he had thought that his reputation as a careful observer and the extreme circumstances would be enough.

August 15, 1934, brought more good weather for diving. Again, Will and Barton crammed themselves into the four-and-a-half foot sphere and sank below the waves.

The fish they saw were unexpectedly large, including a mysterious shape that they were unable to clearly perceive; it may have been a deep-diving whale. Whatever it was, it set the thinking of science on its ear, because it was believed that high pressure and little food made the depths an unsuitable environment for large animals.

This time, they reached a depth of 3,028 feet—more than half a mile down. Captain Sylvester asked Will to return, as there remained only a dozen coils of cable on the winch's drum. The captain was unwilling to take the unknown risk of playing out completely the tremendous weight of both sphere and cable. Will agreed, and within hours he and Barton were back in the sunlit world.

The *National Geographic* article Will wrote based on the dive caused a sensation, especially enhanced by artist Else Boselmann's remarkable paintings of the exotic creatures Will had seen and described. Because a camera that could resist the terrible pressure of such depths hadn't yet been developed, Boselmann's artwork was the best option for depicting the creatures. Months later, his book about the adventure, aptly titled *Half Mile Down*, reached the bestseller lists.

Will never dove so deep again. His new celebrity status plus the constant criticism from detractors wore him out. In 1949, he returned to the tropics, visiting British Guyana, Venezuela, and Trinidad. In 1950 he bought more than 200 acres of tropical forest in Trinidad and named the property Simla. There he continued his studies of the animals, birds, and plants of the jungle, even climbing trees to investigate birds' nests as he had done as a boy. Just as Aldo Leopold had done for the temperate lands, Beebe brought to light the interconnectedness of life in the tropics. (Learn more about Leopold's work in *Earth Heroes: Champions of the Wilderness*.) Many people consider Will the father of neotropical ecology—the ecology of most of Central and South America and the Caribbean area.

Will's writings influenced countless people, both scientists and nonscientists alike. Rachel Carson, Eugenie Clark, and Sylvia Earle are among the scientists who have cited Beebe's influence. His ability to describe what he observed in an entertaining and accessible—while scientifically accurate—way has outlived his detractors.

Will Beebe died June 4, 1962. Of the earnest young man he had mentored, Osborne wrote, "Beebe . . . dared live up to his vision that the wonders of the natural world belonged to everybody."

FAST FACTS

Born: July 29, 1877, Brooklyn, New York

Died: June 4, 1962, Trinidad

Family: Married twice, first to Mary Blair Rice, (divorced), then to Elswyth Thane Ricker.

ACCOMPLISHMENTS:

- Longtime director of the Department of Tropical Research at the New York Zoological Society (now called the Wildlife Conservation Society)
- Received two honorary doctorates
- Reached the depth of more than a half mile below the ocean surface
- Wrote 18 books and numerous scientific papers
- Shifted the concentration of science from the individual organism to the organism's relationships with the all aspects of its habitat
- Pioneered scientific work in marine biology, tropical ecology, and environmental science

RIPPLES OF INFLUENCE:

Famous People Who Influenced William Beebe
Henry David Thoreau, Rudyard Kipling, James Fenimore Cooper, Jules Verne

Famous People Influenced by William Beebe
Rachel Carson, Eugenie Clark, Sylvia Earle, Theodore Roosevelt, Jocelyn Crane, Gloria Hollister Anable (co-founder of the Nature Conservancy), E.O. Wilson, Andrew Dobson

TIMELINE OF IMPORTANT EVENTS

William Beebe's Life

Historical Context

William Beebe's Life	Year	Historical Context
	1865	U.S. Civil War ends
Born July 29	1877	Edison patents the phonograph
	1888	National Geographic Society founded
Publishes first article	1895	X-rays discovered
Begins work at N.Y. Zoological Society	1899	
Marries first wife, Mary Blair Rice	1902	The Teddy Bear is introduced
Publishes *Two Bird Lovers in Mexico*	1905	Audubon Society formed
	1906	Earthquake nearly destroys San Francisco
	1909	Archie Carr born
	1910	Jacques Cousteau born
Beebe and wife divorce	1913	Margaret Wentworth Owings born
Establishes Tropical Research Dept., NY Zoo	1916	World War I fought in Europe
Publishes four-volume work on pheasants	1918	Daylight saving time introduced
	1922	Eugenie Clark born
Marries Elswyth Ricker	1927	First talking movie released
Establishes research station in Bermuda	1928	First Mickey Mouse cartoon released
Meets Otis Barton	1929	Stock market crashes
Makes first bathysphere dive	1930	Worldwide depression begins
Dives over half-mile in bathysphere	1934	Severe Midwest dust storms— "Dust Bowl"
	1935	Sylvia Earle and Roger Payne born
	1941	U.S. enters World War II
Buys Trinidad research station for NY Zoo	1950	Korean War begins
Retires from NY Zoo	1952	Polio vaccine invented
	1956	Iain Kerr born
Dies in Trinidad June 4	1962	Cuban missile crisis

Earth Heroes: Champions of the Ocean

Archie Carr

1909 –1987

The Scientist Who Saved Sea Turtles

"To protect an animal, you have got to know where it is—not once in a while, but all the time."

The six-year-old boy was curious about this odd creature he had found. It looked a lot like the tortoises that he had seen in books, even to the nearsighted way the turtle looked at him. Excited, he tried to grab it, but the box turtle was quicker than he was. It had shut itself up inside its shell before he picked it up.

But the boy was undeterred. He put the turtle down and waited. Slowly, gradually, the turtle peeked out. Excited, the boy shifted, and the turtle ducked back to the safety of its shell.

Time passed. The boy waited. Eventually the turtle thought the coast was clear and slowly extended its head out of the shell. The boy stayed very still—and then quickly slipped a twig into the opening between the turtle's head and its shell. The turtle couldn't withdraw now! The boy later wrote, "Triumphantly, I picked up the vanquished tortoise and, substituting for the stick my own fingertips, tried to widen the breach by a sudden pull. This was a mistake." Howls of pain brought his father running.

The pain in his fingers faded, but Archie Carr never forgot the incident, which "to this day has sustained in me an extra measure of respect for the privacy of others."

Although he learned to respect their privacy—and the power of their shells—Archie would spend his life studying reptiles, the relatives of this box turtle. For him, it was the beginning of a lifelong love affair with the turtles, which would culminate in his keeping one special group, sea turtles, from becoming extinct.

Archie Carr was born June 11, 1909. His father, Archie Carr, Sr., was a minister. His mother, Mimi, had given up a career as concert pianist to become a minister's wife. Instead, she performed at home and gave piano lessons. The house was full of music and the rhythms of his father's sermons. As a result, language and music became as much a part of Archie as his bones.

Young Archie loved to roam the wild places near where he lived, first in Mobile, Alabama, then in Fort Worth, Texas, and then Savannah, Georgia. He kept a sharp eye out for snakes—not because they were dangerous (though some were), but rather because he found them fascinating. Archie was also intrigued by turtles, lizards, and other reptiles and amphibians. Archie walked and watched, and brought particularly interesting specimens home.

People who love the outdoors tend to be tolerant when a bit of the outdoors is brought into their home, so Archie's parents did not object when he collected specimens—although Archie had to be sure to keep the

animals in their cages and not allow them to run loose around the Carr home. His father loved the outdoors and was an avid hunter and fisherman. His mother was, no doubt, used to cleaning and preparing the wild turkey, ducks, and fish that her husband brought home.

Archie as a boy holding two box turtles

Despite his interest in animals, Archie wasn't thinking about making it a career.

When he was a teenager in Savannah, he quickly learned Gullah, a language spoken by African-American dockworkers. Gullah combines English and several different West African languages. Because

Archie's ear for language helped him understand Gullah, unlike other white workers on the docks, he was able to defuse several confrontations before they blew up. Language, it seemed, would be a good choice for a career, so he decided to go to college to become an English teacher.

Archie chose to go to North Carolina and attend Daniel College. However, he contracted an illness called osteomyelitis. The infection attacked the ulna, the smaller of the two bones in his left forearm. Archie had to leave school, and over the next two years, he underwent seven operations. With each operation, the doctors removed more and more bone. In the end, the doctors discovered that the infection had reached his elbow joint. There was no alternative but to do a procedure that would leave the joint frozen in one position. Archie asked them to set the bones at an angle, so the arm would be bent. That way, he figured, he could still hunt and fish.

Archie's struggle with osteomylitis kept him out of college for two years. In 1930, the family moved to Umatilla, Florida, and Archie decided to attend the University of Florida, still planning to be an English teacher. But once again, his plans changed, not due to illness, but by his taking a zoology class.

The University of Florida was well known for its zoology program. The faculty approached the study of animals in a different way than most colleges of the time, emphasizing field work, the testing of hypotheses, and the plants and animals of Florida. Archie was hooked.

Archie later wrote, "As I look back on my junior year in college, I realize that one of the factors that influenced my decision [to change majors] was the hyacinth fauna. It was being able to go out and predictably catch a whole lot of self-effacing little animals that most people don't even know exist." To study these creatures, a group of students wading into the water around a mat of water hyacinths, "all together would start lifting armfuls of hyacinths and throwing them on top of the mat, while at the same time walking slowly toward the bank. . . . By

the time we reached the shore it would be a ponderous, squashy, but coherent bolster."

The students then took the bolster apart plant by plant, shaking each plant over a pan to knock loose the creatures clinging there—a unique community of organisms. Even though such field work entailed bug bites and rashes, Archie changed his major to zoology.

His decision was fortuitous. Fieldwork, the study of Florida's environment, and the testing of hypotheses would mark Archie's work for the rest of his career. Theory was never enough; he tested vigorously every hypothesis he formed, and if it did not hold up, it was abandoned in search of the truth. He never minded getting his hands dirty. And although research would take him around the world, Florida would always hold a special place in his heart as a scientist.

In 1934, he published his first scientific paper, a key to the breeding songs of Florida's frogs, and it provided him with an introduction to some of the leading herpetologists of the day. Two men in particular would influence his life, one in a strongly positive fashion, the other less so: Thomas Barbour of the Museum of Comparative Zoology at Harvard University and Leonard Stejneger of the United States National Museum (now known as the Museum of Natural History at the Smithsonian).

Another influential person arrived in Archie's life at this time. One day, a young woman came to the lab. Marjorie Harris had with her a box of sick quail, small game birds, and she was looking for someone at the university who might help her diagnose what ailed them.

For both Marjorie and Archie, it was love at first sight. They married within a year. Each young naturalist continued to study at the university—Marjorie for her master's degree, Archie for his doctorate. In May, Archie received the first doctorate in zoology ever awarded by the University of Florida.

The Carrs were a great team. Both of them understood and accepted the rigors of fieldwork. Where a nonscientist might have complained about camping, the Carrs camped together contentedly, making themselves at home in the woods, fields, beaches, or marshes. Archie even wore his polka-dot pajamas. On their trips to Mexico, they collected specimens at the request of the Museum of Comparative Zoology at Harvard University. The museum's director, Thomas Barbour, was fond of the young couple and invited them to the museum for the summers. Barbour served as a mentor to both of them, helping them mature and develop as scientists. He also became a very dear friend.

Archie's relationship with Leonard Stejneger, however, was not always so warm and supportive. Stejneger was the leading expert on

Archie and Marjorie camping

turtles in the United States, if not the entire world. For a newly minted scientist to disagree with this grand old man of turtles was unthinkable. But disagree Archie did, concerning the classification of several species of turtles.

In the arcane world of species classification, Archie wanted to make major changes. For example, he wanted to remove the ridley sea turtles from the genus they shared with loggerhead turtles, *Caretta*, and place them in their own genus, *Lepidochelys*. He also determined that the Florida snapping turtle should not be considered a separate species, but rather as a subspecies of a common snapper that was found only in Florida.

For hundreds of years, scientists have been trying to organize living things into some kind of coherent system. Taxonomists, the scientists who specialize in this organization, look at the physical (and, now, genetic) features of organisms to figure out how they might be related and to classify them into groups.

Think of classification as a series of nested boxes: the largest box on the outside is the group called *kingdom*. All animals belong in one kingdom, plants in another, and so on. The second box, *phylum*, divides the kingdom up; for example, animals with spinal cords are grouped in the phylum *Chordata*. The boxes get smaller and smaller until you reach the two most specific groups: the *genus* and the *species*. Genus and species names are used to identify the organism.

However, it's not as simple as it sounds. The scientists may disagree. While today's scientists have DNA analysis to help, during Archie's career, DNA profiles had not yet been developed. Classification is painstaking work and requires tremendous powers of observation. To propose changing the way an animal or plant is classified is a big step, and one that needs to be supported by evidence. Archie had enough evidence to suggest some major changes to turtle classification.

Barbour had been preparing a revision of *A Check List of North American Amphibians and Reptiles*, and had included Archie's changes to Stejneger's taxonomy. Barbour sent it to Stejneger for review, and the older man rejected nearly all of Archie's changes. Archie responded: "I butt-headedly refuse to agree with any of the specific statements [in Stejneger's letter] and with some of the generalizations." A series of exchanges (via letters to Barbour) followed, each scientist adamant in his beliefs regarding the classifications he had assigned the various species, particularly box turtles, snapping turtles, and sea turtles. The debate ended when Stejneger died in 1943, at the age of 92. Archie told his friend Barbour that he hoped the older scientist had not thought badly of him at the end; Barbour assured him that Stejneger had not.

After the United States entered World War II, Archie and Marjorie put research on hold to contribute to the war effort. Archie took a job teaching physics to air corps cadets while Marjorie worked as a nurse's aide. Near the war's end, they were offered an amazing opportunity: to teach at the new Escuela Agrícola Panamericana, an agricultural college in Honduras. He wrote:

> I had just wound up a two-year tour in the Army Air Force Pre-Flight Program at the University of Florida, where I taught elementary physics to impatient cadets and dreamed of a time when I could be a naturalist again. I was ripe for Dr. Popenoe's offer. I took it and went home to tell my wife. She was ready to go before I finished the story.

They would spend five years in Honduras teaching, studying Honduran culture, collecting specimens, and beginning to investigate sea turtles.

In Honduras, and later in other Caribbean nations, Archie learned much about sea turtles from the local people. Unlike other turtles, they have flippers, not feet; their flippers propel them smoothly through the sea. Sea turtles are much larger than other turtles, too. One species, the leatherback, can reach lengths of more than six feet. He also learned that sea turtle eggs, round and white and about as big as a golf ball, were a delicacy, especially when eaten raw with salt and lemon.

Although the closest turtle nesting sites were far from the college, Archie decided to make the journey, first driving eight hours, and then sailing four hours the next day to an island. There, he convinced the men who collected turtle eggs to take the night off.

That night, just after ten o'clock, a female Pacific ridley turtle crawled out of the surf and onto the beach to lay a clutch of eggs.

As he watched the mother turtle's hour-long efforts, he began to wonder: Why did she choose this particular beach? Why, when he shined a light on her after she laid her eggs, did she turn to crawl back up the beach, away from the sea? These questions were the beginning of a lifetime's worth of research and a new understanding of an ancient creature.

In 1952 Archie published his first book, *A Handbook of Turtles,* that summarized everything known about 79 species of turtles from the United States, Canada, and Baja California. It is an exhaustive work. Boring? Not in the least. From the very beginning, where the dedication reads, "To my parents, whose affection withstood the uneasy adolescence of a herpetologist," throughout the entries, the handbook is engaging, lively, and occasionally even funny. If that seems unlikely for a scientific book, it is not at all unlikely for a scientific book written by Archie Carr. Describing a newly hatched musk turtle, he wrote, "...and as is usual with these turtles, it was ready to bite the instant it saw daylight."

Throughout his written works, Archie maintained a comfortable, conversational tone. It is as if he were speaking directly to the reader over a cup of coffee or a glass of soda. He was a man interested in everything, people and animals alike. He was never bored. "I get hot and wet and sleepy. I get impatient, mad, and sometimes hellishly hungry—but not bored."

His second book, *High Jungles and Low* (1953), drew on his experiences in Honduras. But it was his book the very next year that really rang the alarm bells and attracted attention. *The Windward Road* told the world what a desolate future awaited the sea turtle if things did not change. He

Archie Carr

described how the turtles were captured and sold for food and how easy it was, because once turned on their backs, they were entirely helpless.

He told about how the rights to harvest the turtles and their eggs from the *rookery* (breeding) beaches were auctioned off to businessmen and others, called *veladores,* who collected the eggs. "It's a deadly system, and similar systems exploit the nesting beaches all along the coast," he wrote. "Operated at capacity, it would surely destroy the rookery, and the only reason it has not done so is the failure of the veladores to work full-time."

Protecting the turtles was difficult for many reasons. Little was known about their habits. They appeared once a year, laid eggs, and vanished into the great expanse of the ocean. Where did they go? Juvenile turtles were found in Florida, but where they had come from and where they were going was a mystery. How long did it take for the turtles to grow into adults? Would the females lay eggs every year? Since the turtles were viewed as a relatively easily captured food source, what would it take to protect the turtles at their most vulnerable time, when they briefly came ashore to lay their precious eggs?

The Windward Road changed the sea turtle's future. In 1958 Archie received a letter from a reader wanting to help, who asked the intriguing question, "How does one go about starting a movement?" Fortunately the reader was in a position to help. He was Joshua B. Powers, the managing director of a Jamaican newspaper company, and he decided that Archie was right: sea turtles needed protection. Powers set about publicizing Archie's research and concerns to his wealthy friends and also to the people who lived in the areas where turtles nested, laying the groundwork for the organization that would become the Caribbean Conservation Corporation.

Meanwhile, Archie began a research project to test scientifically a belief that had long been held by fishermen in the Caribbean: that the turtles migrated long distances. Archie and his graduate students attached metal tags to more than a thousand turtles. The tags offered a

Earth Heroes: Champions of the Ocean

$5 reward for each tag returned to Archie at the college in Honduras along with information about where the turtle had been caught. The goal was to find out where they went after they left the beaches where they had laid eggs.

Archie also raced to collect turtle eggs before the *veladores* or hungry animals could dig them up. He raised the eggs in captivity. These little turtles beat the odds just by hatching. Archie and his team then released the hatchlings under controlled circumstances, protecting them from the gulls, crabs, and other predators that a tiny turtle must evade before even reaching the water.

His work with the hatchlings led Archie to discoveries that no one could have predicted. He discovered that the baby turtles oriented themselves to the magnetic field of the Earth and, with few exceptions, they swam toward the north.

Archie Carr as an older man with a green sea turtle.

Archie also found that adult female turtles did not choose their nesting beaches at random, but returned to the same beach where they had hatched. If a beach were destroyed or developed, Archie realized, those turtles would have nowhere to nest. To protect the turtles' future, he pressed for the protection of the great nesting beaches.

His work resulted in another popular book, *So Excellent a Fishe*, which drew its name from a colonial-era description of the sea turtle. Although the books were written to be enjoyed, they also had a more important purpose than entertainment. Archie wanted to tell people about how fragile nature was and show them how human actions affected other creatures.

While raising turtles, Archie and Marjorie were also raising five children: Tom, Mimi, Archie III (called Chuck), Stephen, and David. The family settled on a 200-acre farm in Micanopy, Florida. As Marjorie described it, "Well, twenty-five acres was 'farm.' The rest was woods of several kinds, sinkholes, lakes, swamps, and marshes." The farm was a haven for wildlife of all sorts, including an alligator. Archie wrote, "I am

Earth Heroes: Champions of the Ocean

attached to our alligator, deeply so, but she has showed me that a three-hundred pound predator in the front yard is bound to be a mixed blessing at best." Though his research took him near and far, the house in Micanopy remained home.

Over the years, Archie had seen many changes occur in Florida. He began writing a book about his beloved state, but soon realized he did not want to create another "vanishing Eden" kind of book. "I decided simply, 'What the hell, you cry the blues and soon nobody listens.'" Instead, he began to write *A Naturalist in Florida: A Celebration of Eden* to open people's eyes to the richness that existed in the state—complete with stories about his local alligator.

Archie did not live to see *A Naturalist in Florida* when it was finally published in 1994. He developed stomach cancer. But he would receive two more great accolades before he died: the University of Florida's Presidential Medal and the Ecological Society of America's highest honor, the title of Eminent Ecologist. Three weeks later, Archie died at his home in Micanopy, on May 21, 1987.

Archie's legacy lives on. His books and writings are still read. The graduate students he trained lead the current research on sea turtles. The University of Florida established the Archie Carr Center for Sea Turtle Research in 1986. His four sons all entered conservation biology and have been active in the Caribbean Conservation Corporation.

In 1991 the federal government set aside a 248-acre plot of land on the east coast of Archie's beloved Florida and named it the Archie Carr National Wildlife Refuge. The land includes a beach that is a vital nesting ground for the loggerhead sea turtle.

Once called an "archangel" of the conservation movement, Archie Carr's spirit inspires the efforts of those he influenced. When he realized that action needed to be taken, he stepped away from the stereotype of the uninvolved scientist and helped people understand and protect sea turtles. 🍃

FAST FACTS

Born: June 11, 1909, Savannah, Georgia

Died: May 21, 1987, Micanopy, Florida

Wife: Marjorie

Children: Tom, Mimi, Archie III ("Chuck"), Stephen, and David

ACCOMPLISHMENTS:

- Recognized that over-fishing and egg collection threatened the existence of sea turtles

- Conducted research that led to the protection of sea turtles as threatened and endangered species

- Became the world's leading authority on sea turtles

- Inspired the establishment of the Caribbean Conservation Corporation

- Named "Eminent Ecologist" by the Ecological Society of America

- Published more than 120 scientific papers and magazine articles

- Published 10 books

- Won the O. Henry Award for Best Short Story of 1956

RIPPLES OF INFLUENCE:

Famous People who Influenced Archie Carr
Thomas Barbour

Famous People Influenced by Archie Carr
Karen Bjorndal

TIMELINE OF IMPORTANT EVENTS

Archie Carr's Life		Historical Context
Born June 11	1909	Plastic invented
	1910	Jacques Cousteau born
	1913	Margaret Wentworth Owings born
Has encounter with box turtle	1915	World War I fought in Europe
	1922	Eugenie Clark born
Carr family moves to Umatilla, Florida	1930	Worldwide depression begins
Earns bachelor's degree, U of Florida	1932	
Earns master's, publishes paper, marries	1934	Beebe descends half mile in bathysphere
	1935	Sylvia Earle and Roger Payne born
Earns first-ever zoology Ph.D. at U of Florida	1937	Golden Gate Bridge opens
	1941	U.S. enters World War II
First sees a sea turtle lay eggs	1947	First plane flies faster than speed of sound
Publishes *A Handbook of Turtles*	1952	Polio vaccine invented
Publishes *The Windward Road*	1954	Segregated schools ruled illegal in U.S.
Caribbean Conservation Corp. established	1956	Iain Kerr born
	1966	Tierney Thys born
	1972	Marine Mammal Protection Act passed
Archie Carr Ctr. for Sea Turtle Res. created	1986	Nuclear accident occurs at Chernobyl
Dies at home in Micanopy, Florida	1987	
	1989	Berlin Wall falls
Archie Carr Nat'l Wildlife Refuge established	1991	Soviet Union collapses
A Naturalist in Florida published	1994	Nelson Mandela elected S. Africa president

Earth Heroes: Champions of the Ocean

Jacques-Yves Cousteau

1910 – 1997

The Key to the Silent World

"Future generations would not forgive us for having deliberately spoiled their last opportunity, and the last opportunity is today."

The sun and sand of the Mediterranean coast drew hundreds of visitors every summer, including young Jacques' family. His mother and father had rented a seaside cottage, and six-year-old Jacques and his older brother Pierre spent their days exploring the shore.

While Jacques enjoyed the beach, something else caught his eye: the train tracks nearby. Where did the trains come from? And where did they go? While he played with Pierre, his active mind kept returning to the tracks. What would happen if he followed them? Where would they take him? At last he could no longer contain his curiosity. He chose a direction and began walking.

The little boy walked all day. The sun sank lower and lower in the sky. His stomach growled. Eventually, Jacques grew tired. He sat down by the side of the tracks. Once he felt rested, he planned to follow the tracks some more . . .

Suddenly, he was being awakened. *Where have you been? We've been looking for you!* He looked up to see the concerned face of a local police officer.

Jacques went with the officer back to his parents. Although his first expedition had ended prematurely, those train tracks had inspired in Jacques a desire to explore that never left him.

Jacques-Yves Cousteau was born on June 11, 1910, in a small town in France, St. André-de-Cubzac. After Jacques' birth, his family returned to Paris, where his father worked.

Jacques was not healthy as a child. He suffered from chronic enteritis, or inflammation of the small intestine. At the suggestion of his father's employer, his parents arranged for their frail young son to learn to swim. Swimming freed Jacques from the restraints of his illness and opened a new world to him—especially when he began swimming underwater.

Jacques and his family moved to the United States for his father's work and settled in New York City. Jacques learned to rollerskate and play stickball, but of greater consequence to his life was learning to dive. While attending summer camp in Vermont, Jacques got his first taste of swimming underwater. It opened a new world to him, even though he couldn't see clearly because he had no mask or goggles.

When he was thirteen, Jacques bought his first movie camera and began making short films. His obsession with his camera led him to neglect his schoolwork, and his father confiscated it until his grades improved. Jacques was without his camera for only a month. "My films weren't much good," he recalled later. "What I liked was taking the camera apart and developing my own film."

Bright and curious, Jacques enjoyed taking stuff apart. In addition, he had a distinctive ability to see problems and develop a mechanical solution. A couple of years earlier, he had devised a crane that would unload ships more efficiently. An engineer who saw Jacques' model told his father to patent the design.

Many of the things he wanted to do—such as swim freely underwater unencumbered by heavy diving helmets, and shoot underwater photographs and films—had never been done before. He would have to invent the equipment that would make his dreams a reality.

When it came time to choose a career, he decided to join the military, mostly because it would allow him to travel. He graduated from the

French Naval Academy and was shipped off to China. There he surveyed the land and made maps—and spent his free time filming the people and places he saw.

When he returned to France, he prepared to enter pilot training. But one night before he entered the program, the car Jacques was driving went off the road and rolled over and over. With one arm paralyzed and the other broken in five places, Jacques struggled to get to a nearby farmhouse. It was two o'clock in the morning.

"Go away!" cried the lady of the house.

"Madame, if you saw me, you would not say that," Jacques replied.

The lady took a look and let him in.

The broken arm became infected and doctors wanted to amputate it. Jacques refused. Instead, he followed his own program of rehabilitation. After eight months, he could move a finger; after 10 months, he could move two fingers and his wrist. He began to swim every day, and the exercise helped the arm get stronger. Although the arm remained slightly twisted for the rest of his life, he regained its use. "It was a test for me," he later said.

During this time of recuperation, he swam often at Le Mourillon Bay, on France's Mediterranean coast. While swimming there one day, he met a young woman, Simone Melchior. After a year-long courtship, they married in 1937, and would have two sons, Jean-Michel and Philippe. Simone was Jacques' partner for the next 50 years, diving alongside him and helping to keep Jacques and his dreams afloat, until she died in 1990.

Another life-changing event happened at Le Mourillon. A fellow naval officer, Philippe Tailliez, loaned Jacques a pair of goggles, a precursor to today's diving masks. "I was astounded by what I saw . . . rocks covered with green, brown, and silver forests of algae and fishes unknown to me, swimming in crystalline water," he later wrote in his book, *The Silent World*.

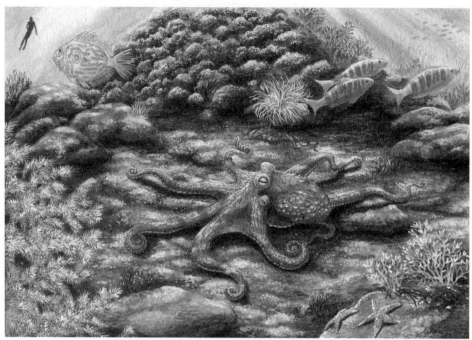

When Jacques first wore goggles while swimming in the Mediterranean, it revealed an entire world of fish, anemone, starfish, octopus, and much more. He wondered what he could do to be able to dive deeper.

Sometimes we are lucky enough to know that our lives have been changed, to discard the old, embrace the new, and run headlong down an immutable course. It happened to me at Le Mourillon on that summer's day, when my eyes were opened on the sea.

What he saw clearly at Le Mourillon that day lit a fire of curiosity in him. If the goggles allowed him to see so much within just a few feet of the surface, what wonders would he be able to see if he could dive deeper?

He began diving regularly with goggles, and his activities did not go unnoticed. By this time World War II had started. Germany had invaded France and occupied it, and soon soldiers from Germany's ally, Italy, also arrived. The French navy asked him to keep a keen lookout, particularly when diving near any undersea equipment belonging to the occupying German and Italian forces. Although the occupying forces questioned him periodically about his diving activities, they never realized that Jacques was more than just a goggling enthusiast—he was a spy!

Jacques worked with the French underground, a group of people fighting against the Germans, as part of a naval assignment. One night he arranged for a group of resistance members to impersonate Italian officers, break into an office, and photograph the code book and the cipher keys hidden in the office safe. At the last minute, one man backed out, so Jacques had to go in his place. Not one of the imposters spoke enough Italian to fool the guards, but fortunately, they bluffed their way in without a word. Getting the safe open took an excruciating 45 minutes. It took another four nerve-wracking hours to record the code book and the cipher keys on film before they could leave.

He never learned what became of the information they gathered that night, but he learned more about taking risks—that they are not to be undertaken lightly. Yet taking risks was an inherent part of what became Jacques' chosen career—exploring the underwater world and bringing its grandeur to people's awareness.

Through Tailliez, Jacques met another goggling enthusiast, Fréderic "Didi" Dumas. The three men formed a lifelong friendship. They shared the desire to swim freely underwater, without using the heavy diving helmets that connected the diver with an air pump above the surface. Jacques was experimenting with ways to take photographs underwater. Why not also apply his clever mind to developing a better way to dive?

One of his first diving contraptions was made from part of a gas mask, a tank of compressed oxygen, and a motorcycle-tire inner tube. A soda-lime canister from the gas mask would remove the carbon dioxide from the air that the diver exhaled. A gunsmith on his naval ship built it for him, and two sailors agreed to watch him as he tested his device.

"Swimming twenty-five feet down with the oxygen apparatus was the most serene thrill I have had in the water," he later wrote. "Silent and alone in a trancelike land, one was accepted by the sea."

Enchanted, he dove deeper. But suddenly, Jacques went into convulsions. Unknown to him, at that depth, the pure oxygen he was breathing became toxic. He ripped off his weight belt and floated to the surface, where the sailors hauled him into the waiting boat. He replaced the soda-lime canister, which he thought might have been contaminated, and tried again. And again, a violent convulsion gripped him. "I came very near drowning," he wrote. "It was the end of my interest in oxygen." Clearly, an effective and safe diving device would require more than just mechanical genius. The mixture of gases breathed by the diver had to be rethought as well.

How could a diving device provide normal air to a diver without the diver having to control it manually? A diving device did exist that used compressed air, but the diver had to open and close a valve every time he took a breath. But when a diver had to concentrate on breathing, it diverted his attention away from the wonders before him.

It was a knotty problem, but Simone came to the rescue. Her father was an executive at France's leading natural gas company, and he introduced Jacques to Émile Gagnan, a talented engineer. When Jacques described what he wanted—a device that could provide a diver with air without his having to think about it—Gagnan showed him a valve he was working on to deliver cooking gas into car engines in place of war-rationed gasoline. With some modifications, they created the first automatic regulator, which provided a steady, regular flow of safe air to the diver.

Later generally known as SCUBA gear, the Aqua-lung was invented by Jacques working with Emile Gagnan. It opened up the world of underwater diving.

Combined with compressed air tanks and carefully positioned hoses, the regulator made up the prototype of their diving apparatus, which they called the Aqualung. Gagnan and Cousteau patented the Aqualung in 1943, and Jacques spent the next summer thoroughly testing it with Tailliez and Dumas. Although Cousteau and Gagnan called their invention the Aqualung, it is now commonly called "SCUBA," an acronym for "Self-Contained Underwater Breathing Apparatus."

Together, the men made more than 500 dives with the Aqualung. It allowed them to move underwater more freely than ever before—as freely as a fish! Simone dove with the Aqualung, too, as did little Philippe and Jean-Michel, ages five and six, using smaller versions of the equipment. However, the boys were so excited by what they could see that they kept trying to talk, even with the regulators in their mouths. "I seized the waterlogged infants and hauled them out of the water," Cousteau said later, and admonished them that under the sea was a "silent world"—one that should not be disturbed by little boys' chatter!

Although the difficulty of oxygen toxicity had been solved, the Aqualung was not without its dangers. The men kept diving deeper and deeper. At around 200 feet down, Didi found he felt drunk, giddy, and enraptured with everything around him. Although he did not know it at the time, he was suffering nitrogen narcosis, or "rapture of the deep." Only by fighting to keep your wits about you can you survive the rapture of the deep. Of "rapture," Jacques wrote:

> I am personally quite receptive to nitrogen rapture. I like it and fear it like doom. It destroys the instinct of life. Tough individuals are not overcome as soon as [less hearty] persons like me, but they have difficulty extricating themselves. Intellectuals get drunk early and suffer acute attacks on all the senses, which demand hard fighting to overcome.

The Aqualung not only gave scientists and researchers a new tool for ocean exploration, it opened the wonders of the ocean to anyone who was trained to use it properly. Today more than 40,000 people worldwide are certified in SCUBA diving every month.

The Aqualung allowed Jacques and his men to take photographs and make films underwater more easily than ever before. Jacques did not invent underwater photography; the first images had been taken in 1893, years before his birth. Now with the Aqualung, the filmmakers were free from the hoses and heavy helmets. They learned more about how light acts underwater, which affects both the colors of objects and our perception of the sizes and distances of things we see. Jacques discovered that color movies could be made at 127 feet down. He also found out that, because of the way light refracts through water and a diver's mask, a six-foot-long shark appears to be nine feet long!

Now that he had the Aqualung, Jacques knew that he could dive almost anywhere. But the problem of getting there remained. He had his eye on a ship he had seen docked in Malta—a former British minesweeper, a wooden-hulled boat that was being used as a ferry. But a ship was a huge expense.

Again Simone came to the rescue. When they were out at dinner one evening, she began chatting with the people at the next table. One of the men turned out to be Thomas Guinness, owner of the Irish brewery, and he wanted to support ocean exploration.

Thanks to him, Jacques was able to buy the ship he wanted, the *Calypso*. (See silhouette of the ship at the beginning of this chapter.) The ship would be his home base for the next five decades.

Soon after obtaining *Calypso*, Jacques published his first book, *The Silent World*. In it, he lyrically described the wonder of diving beneath the surface of the sea, and described the development of the Aqualung and his undersea photography. The book, written with Dumas and American journalist Jim Dugan, was a hit, and has sold more than five million copies and been translated into 20 languages.

Jacques made a film two years later, also called *The Silent World*, after taking *Calypso* on a 13,800-mile ocean journey. The film premiered

Jacques opened the undersea world for millions of people. The Calypso (in background) was his home base for research, diving, and filming.

at the prestigious Cannes Film Festival and received the Palme d'Or, the festival's highest honor. It then went on to win an Oscar from the American Academy of Motion Picture Arts and Sciences in 1956.

The film marked the beginning of a new role for the naval officer, inventor, explorer, and former spy—teacher to the world. During the 1960s, Jacques' films premiered on American television, making his discoveries accessible to more people than ever before. His TV series, *The Undersea World of Jacques Cousteau,* ran for eight seasons. *Undersea World* made Cousteau and his *Calypso* household names as viewers tuned in to see the adventures of the tall, thin French captain in his trademark watch cap, along with his sons and crew. Thanks to him, people were able to see brilliant reef fish and corals, huge and mysterious whales, amusing seals, and sleek sharks—all in their natural environment, a privilege that had been available only to divers.

To make his films, Jacques invented many tools that allowed him and his crew to get closer to the creatures of the sea. The human body has limits, especially in the unnatural environment of the ocean. To dive deep safely, divers needed protection—a craft to ride in. In the 1930s, William Beebe and Otis Barton had descended to depths of a half mile, off the coast of Bermuda, in the bathysphere that Barton had designed. French inventor Auguste Piccard improved on their design and created the deep-diving bathyscaphe, *Trieste*.

Both the bathysphere and bathyscaphe were incredible advances, but Jacques wanted something different: a quick, maneuverable undersea device with which to explore the depths. So he devised the "diving saucer." The first version was lost in 1953, but in 1959, the *DS-2* was launched. Its purpose was not to reach the incredible depths that the *Trieste* had reached. Rather, the diving saucer gave human divers a hard outer shell that could protect them at depths of 1,000 feet.

Some people, including many scientists, pooh-poohed Jacques' films and books. These critics said that the narration, recorded by Jacques himself, was not scientific, but instead was a breathless exclamation of wonder. Cousteau was also criticized for attributing human feelings to, or *anthropomorphizing*, the creatures he observed, as in this selection from his book, *The Whale: Mighty Monarch of the Sea* (1972):

> . . . a baby whale left its mother's side to rub against *Polaris III*. The mother immediately went after the calf, pushed it far away from the ship—and then struck it several times with her flippers. The blows had every appearance of being slaps, and they were obviously administered in order to teach the baby not to confuse a ship's hull with a mother's stomach.

Yet Cousteau had never pretended to be a research scientist, bound by the rules of publication and scientific detachment. He was a filmmaker with an unabashed and unapologetic affection for the ocean and its

Jacques used his influence as a celebrity to honor young environmentalists as "Eco Stars." One such star was Kristin Joy Pratt, who at age 15 wrote and illustrated a children's picture book, A Swim through the Sea.

creatures. And the public loved his way of presenting what he and the crew of the *Calypso* observed.

Each film and book met with an eager and receptive audience, and the money that Jacques earned helped support the *Calypso's* journeys. Jacques found himself becoming part of the popular culture. Comedians fondly imitated his thick French accent, biographers wrote his life story, and songwriters penned musical tributes to the man and his ship. He received many honors and awards.

The inventions, books, and films were part of his larger role as a teacher. As President John F. Kennedy said in 1961 when he presented the captain with the National Geographic Society's Gold Medal, "To earthbound man he gave the key to the silent world."

After teaching for years about the wonders of the ocean, Jacques turned his attention to publicizing the need to protect the sea. In 1973, he established the Cousteau Society, a nonprofit organization with the goal of teaching people about the ocean while working for the protection and conservation of the world's most precious places. He also used his celebrity status to encourage young environmentalists, honoring some as "Eco Stars."

In 1985 a second vessel, the *Alcyone*, joined Jacques' team of explorers. It was specially outfitted with "turbosails" to use wind power to supplement the engines. In 1996 the *Calypso* sank in Singapore harbor when it was accidentally rammed by a barge. The *Alcyone* became Jacque's primary research vessel.

During his years of diving, he had seen terrible changes take place in the ocean. He wanted to alert people to how their actions on land affected life in the ocean. When he testified before Congress, he said, "People do not realize that all pollution ends up in the sea. The Earth is less polluted. It is washed by rain, which carries everything into the oceans, where life has diminished by 40 percent in twenty years."

Jacques, aboard the Alcyone, watches with amusement when a sea lion rests on the inflatable craft.

Earth Heroes: Champions of the Ocean

Pollution and development were deadly for the living sea. When a third factor—over-fishing—was added to the equation, Jacques feared for the continued survival of the ocean world. He was able to use his celebrity status to speak for the environment. Not only could he tell people what was happening in the oceans, but with his films, he could show them. He said that he was most proud of his work that helped to protect Antarctica, the Amazon, and Alaska. "All these things have been hard won," he said. "And we did it, and I am proud of it."

Jacques died of a heart attack June 25, 1997. Just four months later, the Jacques Cousteau National Estuarine Research Reserve opened in New Jersey.

The Cousteau Society continues Jacques' work today, under the leadership of his widow, Francine Cousteau. She coordinated the effort to raise the *Calypso* from where it sank in Singapore and return it to France for repairs.

The water helped heal Jacques Cousteau from childhood frailty, and later helped heal his terrible automobile injury as a young man. In return, "the Captain" led the way in telling the story that our ocean planet is now also in need of healing. His children and grandchildren carry on the work he began.

The curious little boy didn't follow the train tracks too far away from the sea, after all.

Fast Facts

Born: June 11, 1910, St. André-de-Cubzac, France

Died: June 25, 1997, Paris, France

Wife: Simone (died); Francine (second wife)

Children: Jean-Michel, Philippe, Diane, Pierre-Yves

ACCOMPLISHMENTS:

- Invented the Aqualung with Émile Gagnan
- Produced more than 140 films
- Introduced millions of people to the wonders of the ocean
- Wrote 34 books, for adults and children
- Led movement to prevent the dumping of nuclear waste in the Mediterranean
- Was instrumental in developing a diving saucer and the turbosail system
- Received the gold medal from the National Geographic Society in 1961
- Received the United Nations' International Environmental Prize in 1977
- Received the U.S. Medal of Freedom in 1985
- Inducted into the Académie Française in 1989
- Inducted into the Television Academy Hall of Fame in 1987

Famous People Influenced by Jacques Cousteau
President John F. Kennedy, Larry Madin (senior scientist at the Woods Hole Oceanographic Institution), Bruce Robison (senior scientist at the Monterey Bay Aquarium Research Institute), Charles Caraguel, John Denver

Timeline

Jacques Cousteau's		Life Historical Context
	1909	Archie Carr born
Born June 11	1910	Boy Scouts of America founded
	1913	Margaret Wentworth Owings born
	1915	World War I fought in Europe
	1922	Eugenie Clark born
Buys first movie camera	1923	Talking movies invented
	1930	Worldwide depression begins
	1934	Beebe descends half mile in bathysphere
	1935	Sylvia Earle and Roger Payne born
Marries first wife, Simone Melchior	1937	Japan invades China
Son Jean-Michel born	1938	Ballpoint pen invented
Son Philippe born	1940	First U.S. freeway opens in Los Angeles
Patents Aqualung with Émile Gagnan	1943	World War II fought
Obtains ship that becomes *Calypso*	1950	Sen. McCarthy on communist witch hunt
	1952	Polio vaccine invented
Produces first version of diving saucer	1953	First successful open-heart surgery
Wins Oscar for *The Silent World*	1956	Iain Kerr born
Directs Musée Oceanographique, Monaco	1957	Russia launches first satellite, Sputnik
Awarded Nat'l Geo. Society's Gold Medal	1961	Peace Corps established
	1962	Beebe dies; Cuban missile crisis
Releases *World Without Sun* and *Voyage*	1965	U.S. sends troops to Vietnam
	1966	Tierney Thys born
TV launch, *Undersea World of Jacques Cousteau*	1968	R.F. Kennedy, M.L. King, Jr. assassinated
	1972	U.S. law protects whales in US waters
Establishes the Cousteau Society	1973	U.S. withdraws from Vietnam
Produces *Oasis in Space* TV series	1977	*Star Wars* movie released
	1979	Sylvia Earle dives deep in Jim suit
TV launch, *Rediscovery of the World I*	1986	Nuclear accident occurs at Chernobyl
	1987	Archie Carr dies
TV launch, *Rediscovery of the World II*	1992	First Earth summit held in Rio de Janeiro
Calypso sinks in Singapore	1996	Sheep cloned from adult cells
Dies of heart attack, June 25	1997	Hong Kong returns to Chinese rule
Calypso raised, taken to France for repairs	2008	Obama first African-American president

Earth Heroes: Champions of the Ocean

Margaret Wentworth Owings

1913 – 1999

Friend of the Otter, and Others

"What we do to the otter, we do to ourselves."

A nine-year-old girl hurried down the road to the beach. The Pacific Ocean rushed over the sand making a soft hissing sound. Gulls wheeled above, adding their squawking to the ocean's song.

Margaret had not come to the beach to play. She was on a mission. She ignored the gulls and picked her way out over the rocks to a tide pool. She knelt down on the rocks, slippery with algae, and peered down through the crystal water. The bottom of the tidal pool was a riot of color. "They had pink coralline algae in these pools," she remembered later. "And then purple and vermillion sea urchins, and the anemones, and the snails." The animals and their colors intrigued the girl, who had an artist's eye and a naturalist's heart. "It was the most wonderful discovery in my life, and it somehow sealed my connection with the sea."

Margaret Wentworth was born April 29, 1913, in Berkeley, California. Her parents, William and Jean, had recently moved to California from Boston. They both loved nature. William owned a successful printing company and furniture business before retiring in 1929. He supported Richard St. Barbe Baker's campaign to protect ancient redwood trees in California (see the chapter about Baker in *Earth Heroes: Champions of the Wilderness*), and retirement gave him more time to work with the Save-the-Redwoods League, among other environmental causes.

Soon the family moved to Thousand Oaks, near Los Angeles. At the time, Thousand Oaks was largely undeveloped. Three other houses stood on the same road as the Wentworths' home, and her family owned large fields across the road. "My brother and I grew up among trees," Margaret remembered. They walked through groves of eucalyptus and oak on their way to school.

Yet Margaret wasn't well. Although it would not be diagnosed for decades, she had diabetes. She loved art, drawing the animals and plants around her. She also loved to read, and one book in particular made a strong impression. It was called *Lightfoot the Deer*. She read it over and over. "It probably did a lot to color my strong feeling for wildlife and to protect wildlife from hunters," she said later.

After high school, Margaret decided to attend college and major in art. After earning her bachelor's degree at Mills College in 1934, she went on to graduate school at Harvard University's Fogg Art Museum. There she met Malcolm Millard, a young man from Chicago. They fell in love and were married in 1937.

Although Margaret may have been happy to be married, her delight quickly turned to despair when they moved in with Malcolm's family, which was much more restrained and conservative than her own. "It deadened me and took all the creative things out of me," she recalled. Although the couple had a daughter, Wendy, the marriage ended in divorce.

Margaret and Wendy moved to New Mexico, where she rented a small house. One of their neighbors was Nathaniel Owings, a famous architect.

In December 1953, Margaret and Nathaniel married. While courting, they visited Big Sur, a magnificent place on the ocean south of San Francisco. Margaret had always loved the area, and Nat quickly fell in love with it, too. Big Sur is a coastline where the cliffs meet the ocean in sheer drops of hundreds of feet. They decided that Big Sur was the ideal place for them. Of Big Sur, Margaret wrote:

May I speak of those moments after sunrise, when the mist is rising from the sea and the fog is fingering the canyons of Big Sur? Each day lies before us, guarding our lasting plans for continuity. And the sea, that life-giving support, lies quietly below us in its undisturbed immensity. At times one hears only a broad current of sound, too subtle for human ears to define. Is it the sea otter twisting the kelp fronds to make a hammock for rafting—or perhaps the flap of a cormorant's wings touching the water as they dive?

Nathaniel designed and built a house that Margaret named "Wild Bird." The house, which still stands on the 55-acre homestead, features balconies around the outside that allow for views of the coast and the white sand beach 600 feet below.

Margaret's husband Nathaniel, an architect, designed "Wild Bird," which served as a constant inspiration as well as her home and headquarters for wildlife advocacy campaigns.

The view from Wild Bird gave Margaret an increased appreciation for wild things. Peregrines and red-tailed hawks swooped along the cliffs as seagulls screeched at them. Foxes, ring-tailed cats, and other wild creatures lived there as they always had. Sea lions lolled about on the beach.

When they arrived, Big Sur was home to few people. But there were rumblings of development that threatened the unique beauty of the place. The nearby town of Carmel planned to build more than 1000 houses on a stretch of land jutting into the ocean. The land had previously been used for coal mining, whaling, and abalone canning.

In 1952, Margaret and several other residents raised funds to purchase the property. As a child Margaret had seen such a strategy work when her father protected a nearby eucalyptus grove by buying it from the owner. And when her father was involved with the Save-the-Redwoods League, they protected land by purchasing it. The purchase protected the land, which eventually became part of Point Lobos State Park.

At the time, the sea lion population near Big Sur had increased considerably in just a few years. Declaring that the mammals were eating so many fish that they were harming the commercial fishing industry, in 1959 a state senator proposed to use depth bombs to kill about three-quarters of the sea lions that lived on the coast. At first, Margaret recalled, "I cried." Then she went into action. She appealed to people she knew— Ansel Adams, Nicholas Roosevelt, Samuel F.B. Morse, Warren Olney, Laurence Rockefeller, Roy Chapman Andrews, and Starker Leopold (son of the great conservationist Aldo Leopold; see the chapter in *Earth Heroes: Champions of the Wilderness*)—to write letters protesting the plan. She helped form a group, The Committee to Save the Sea Lions, that called for a scientific study to find out how great an impact the sea lions had on the fish population. Just 21 days after the senator proposed his plan, it was defeated.

But the battle to save the sea lions wasn't over. The senator introduced a new bill that was essentially a ploy to throw Margaret off the trail. It still gave California sea lions the death sentence—except for the ones near Margaret's home! The senator had badly misjudged Margaret.

> He was ridiculous to think that if this bill said the beach below my house would be out of bounds, and Point Lobos would be out of bounds, that that would be all I'd want. That just made my hair stand straight up.

She redoubled her efforts. She called and wrote to newspaper editors to publicize the state's plans. At that time there were no videos or TV nature specials about sea lions to educate people about them. The success or failure of the effort depended on the written word. And failure was not an option. "The thing really that stopped it with many people was the fact that they were talking about dynamiting the sea lions. The thought that it would make the beaches unpleasant is what stopped it . . . Isn't that incredible?"

Margaret organized to save sea lions in California. A state senator, convinced that they were eating too many fish, proposed to kill most of them with underwater explosives.

Margaret discovered that she had a gift with words, and she became a strong voice in support of nature—even though that voice was sometimes not welcome.

In 1963, she was named to the California Park Commission. Headlines read, "Crusader named to park board." She worked to protect redwoods from highway development until she resigned in 1969. She was the only woman on the commission during that time.

Sometimes Margaret heard the sound of a female mountain lion (or *cougar*) near Wild Bird. One day she learned that it had been shot and killed. The man who killed the cat was being treated like a hero. And he was given a bounty—a payment of money by the government—for killing an "unwanted" animal. "At that point, I knew very little about mountain lions," she explained.

What she did know stemmed from one night when she was a child. Tucked into bed yet still awake, she heard a mighty scream outside the house—the scream of a mountain lion. The lion's voice frightened her but also inspired a sense of awe for the great cats. Margaret never forgot that night.

She approached a state senator and asked him to help get the bounty repealed. At the time, bounties were considered by some people to be an effective means for controlling predators. She called on people who had helped her before with the sea lion cause—Adams, Rockefeller, Roosevelt—as well as other prominent people, such as Henry Fairfield Osborne of the New York Zoological Society, and Rachel Carson.

Together, they succeeded in repealing the bounty on mountain lions. But for the rest of her life, Margaret would fight to outlaw the killing of mountain lions altogether in California.

Her work to protect the trees, sea lions, and mountain lions proved that the government would listen and respond if enough people spoke out. As long as people were informed, they cared mightily and demanded action.

Earth Heroes: Champions of the Ocean

Yet Margaret's greatest cause still lay ahead: the sea otter. Sea otters are the smallest of all marine mammals.

Mother sea otters often hold their babies on their stomachs as they float, and they have endearing, whiskery faces. They live in coastal waters, where they dive for sea urchins, snails, and other shellfish. To open their hard-shelled meals, they float on their backs and place a flat stone on their bellies. Then they hit the shellfish on the rock over and over until the shell breaks. Or, they may use the rock as a hammer to open the shell.

But unfortunately for the otters, their luxurious, waterproof fur was almost their undoing. Fur hunters began to kill the otters for their pelts in the mid-1700s. By 1903, when they had become scarce, a single skin could fetch more than a thousand dollars—making the sea otter's fur the most expensive of any mammal's. By 1911, only about a thousand otters survived in the entire world. A southern subspecies that lived in California was believed extinct. However, a few—between fifty and a hundred—had survived, and escaped human detection until 1938.

"When the otters were first rediscovered, I was living in Illinois," Margaret recalled. "It came out in *Life* magazine with a big picture of otters. I studied them. I had no idea what this was going to do to my life."

Sea otters were almost exterminated for their luxurious fur, and fishermen wanted to eliminate them as fishing competitors. Margaret rallied public support to protect them.

When she returned to California in 1949, she saw her first otter. She wrote:

> ... in a towering, transparent wave that was curling inward to plunge and break in this thin, crystal sheeting of water against the evening sun, my first sea otter stretched horizontal in silhouette for one hammock-swung moment.

Not everyone was as happy to see the otters as Margaret. During the 1950s and 1960s, abalone fishermen became increasingly convinced that the otters were stealing "their" shellfish. An abalone is a kind of mollusk, related to clams and snails. Its shell is a source of iridescent mother of pearl, and the abalone meat is a popular seafood. The fishermen maintained that the sea otters were eating too many of the abalones. The conflict grew over the years until finally the fishermen demanded that the state do something about the otters, which they viewed as unwelcome competition for a limited number of abalones.

In 1968, a friend invited her to attend a committee hearing of the California Senate at which abalone fishermen planned to make their case. During the hearing, she asked herself, "Am I going really to start to work on this?"

The meeting grew loud. People were shouting to be heard. Margaret stood and said that the population of the otters had declined. A man jumped up on a table and retorted, "I know what you're thinking! You're thinking that we shot them. But I want to tell you that it's mighty hard to shoot an otter from a rocking boat." It seems that he had tried!

The meeting concluded with the committee's decision to form a citizens' committee to study the issue further. Margaret decided that the sea otters needed allies, and she would be one of them. She founded another conservation group, Friends of the Sea Otter.

A state senator introduced a bill to authorize the killing of any sea otters found outside of the California Sea Otter Refuge. Margaret fought back. She created a flyer and illustrated it with a photograph of a mother sea otter and her pup. She mailed the flyer to newspaper editors and to Sierra Club members. It explained the meaning of the language of the bill, including the word "taken," which was a synonym for "killed." The flyer also noted that the otters range nearly 50 miles outside of the refuge.

"It just caught hold like wildfire," she said. School children from around the state wrote to the senator, urging him not to kill the otters.

When it came time for a vote on the bill, Margaret and Nat gathered scientists who knew about otters and flew them to Sacramento. Laypeople came too. "Nat hired a Greyhound bus and all the excited otter people filled it. They had placards. They had pins with a picture of an otter on it, and Friends of the Sea Otter written under it. . . . It couldn't have been more successful." The bill was withdrawn. The otters, for the moment, were safe.

Behind the scenes, Margaret's husband Nat helped with the campaigns.

Sea otters became popular thanks to Margaret's writings, and became even more so as film stars! In 1971, Jacques Cousteau, his son Philippe, and the crew of the *Calypso* arrived in Monterey to make a film about the sea otters called *The Unsinkable Sea Otter.* Another filmmaker, Bill Bryan, also publicized the charming little animals in his film, *Clowns of the Sea.* Yet another film, *Back from Extinction,* was made by Jim Mattison. The three films publicized the otter's charm and playfulness. Audiences loved them.

In 1972, a bill was proposed in Congress to protect sea otters, sea lions, seals, whales, and other sea mammals. "We took a very active part in this," Margaret recalled. "We went and testified . . . We went around and met all the congressmen." In addition, 75,000 people signed a petition asking that the sea otter be listed as an endangered species. Because of broad public support for sea mammals, they succeeded: the

Marine Mammal Protection Act became law. Under the law, no one may kill, harass, capture, or even approach a marine mammal unless they have a special permit issued by the federal government. The next year, the protection was reinforced when Congress passed the Endangered Species Act.

When Margaret started the Friends of the Sea Otter, she ran the organization from her own house, Wild Bird. But its membership was growing rapidly, and the organization was no longer a dining-room-table kind of enterprise. Margaret realized that it needed to move into a real office, and employ a full-time scientist on staff.

In 1975, Dr. Betty Davis, a zoologist, became the new executive secretary of Friends of the Sea Otter. She expanded the organization's focus to include not just the otter itself but also its environment. For

For many years, Friends of the Sea Otter and other campaigns operated out of Margaret's spectacular home, "Wild Bird."

example, otters help protect the great kelp forests by eating sea urchins, which nibble away the holdfasts of the kelp.

Although otters now had federal protection, the battle was still not over. Oil spills, for example, could be disastrous to the otters. Unlike other sea mammals, sea otters don't have an insulating layer of fat under their skin; they depend on their fur to keep warm. If an otter becomes covered in oil, the oil ruins the fur's insulating properties. The cold water soaks down to the otter's skin and its body temperature falls. If it gets too cold, it dies.

Earth Heroes: Champions of the Ocean

In 1980 there was a proposal to build an oil terminal on the California coast that would be likely to expose otters to oil spills. Supertankers would be allowed to unload oil there. A supertanker is a ship built specifically to carry oil—lots of oil. One supertanker can carry approximately two million gallons of crude oil. The supertankers that would have docked at that particular terminal were not well maintained and had poorly trained crews. The question wasn't *if* a spill would happen, but *when*. "I got really worked up and excited about it," Margaret said.

Margaret went into action. She invited leaders of the California energy industry to lunch at Wild Bird. She also invited a former oil tanker captain who knew the threats the big ships posed. Although the business leaders made no promises, the Friends of the Sea Otter had attracted their attention. In addition, its members testified at government hearings. The efforts of the Friends of the Sea Otter were rewarded in June 1980, when the U.S. Army Corps of Engineers refused to allow construction of the terminal. The engineers said, "This oil is the greatest threat to sea otters, and we have made this decision because of the otters."

In 1983, Margaret received the Audubon Medal in recognition of her conservation work.

The next year, Nat passed away. Margaret lost her greatest ally and staunchest supporter. Yet she continued the work they had done together, continuing to lead the Friends of the Sea Otter until 1990.

Her words flowed profusely and passionately, as in this description of otters that she penned as an epilogue of a book, *The Sea Otter*, by Roy Nickerson:

> . . . [O]ne perceives another subtlety through the magnified clarity of the water—the flowing grace in motion of a sea otter, a southern sea otter, exploring with its forepaws and navigating with its webbed hind feet. And now, another otter bursts through the pattern of kelp, whiskers fanning out as it parts the fronds while holding between its forepaws a clutch of mussels ripped from nearshore rocks below the surface.

The privilege of watching this smallest of marine mammals from the shore offers each of us a personal reunion with life in the sea. Gradually, as we familiarize ourselves with the little otter, the whole ecology of the coast commences to unfold. An empathy is exchanged between us as the sea otter plays and splashes, alertly raising its head to focus upon us with curiosity before it turns with a flip and somersaults beneath the surface. This vitality draws people to the edge of the sea, its sands, its promontories, as well as its underwater world in which the otter pursues a key role.

While fighting for the sea otter, Margaret had been involved in many other environmental causes. From 1968-1969, she was a member of the National Parks Foundation Board, at the invitation of President Lyndon B. Johnson. She was also deeply involved with the Sierra Club, the African Wildlife Leadership Foundation, Defenders of Wildlife, the Environmental Defense Fund, and the California Mountain Lion

Margaret loved to be in that special, vibrant place where land and sea meet, and dedicated her life to its preservation, especially of the unique creatures living there.

Preservation Foundation. Her conservation work consumed her, leaving her little time for art.

Margaret collected her lifetime of writings and artwork. The resulting book, published by the Monterey Bay Aquarium, was called *Voice from the Sea*. In it she celebrated not only nature, but also the many people she had worked with on conservation efforts—everyone from politicians and First Ladies to actors and scientists. And of course, she wrote about her beloved Nat. The book was published just a month before her death. She died at her home, Wild Bird, in January, 1999.

In the sea below the house and on the cliffs nearby, her legacy lives on. Mountain lions walk silently through the woods. Peregrine falcons raise their chicks in cliff-side nests. Canyon wrens build their nests in places safe from the falcons. Sea lions call to each other in rough voices. And rescued from the edge of oblivion, sea otters wrap themselves in kelp to keep from drifting off while they nap. As Margaret said:

What we do to the otter, we do to the chain of life.
What we do to the otter, we do to ourselves.

Fast Facts

Born: April 29, 1913, Berkeley, California

Died: January 21, 1999, Big Sur, California

Husband: Malcolm Millard (divorced); Nathaniel Owings

Children: Wendy (with Malcolm Millard); stepchildren Nathaniel Jr., Natalie, Jennifer, and Emily

ACCOMPLISHMENTS:

- Prevented the extinction of the southern sea otter
- Fought to protect sea lions
- Ended California's bounty on mountain lions
- Prevented the clearing of redwood groves
- Founded Friends of the Sea Otter
- Was an honorary member of the California State Park Rangers Association
- Served as a trustee of the Environmental Defense Fund, Defenders of Wildlife, and Sierra Club
- Received the Lifetime Achievement Award, Children's Health Environmental Coalition (1996)
- Received the United Nations Environmental Gold Medal (1988)

RIPPLES OF INFLUENCE:

Famous People Who Influenced Margaret Wentworth Owings
John Muir, Frank Wentworth, Rachel Carson, Richard St. Barbe Baker, Wallace Stegner, George Schaller

Famous People Influenced by Margaret Wentworth Owings
Robert Redford, Ansel Adams, President Lyndon B. Johnson, Jane Goodall, Jennifer Owings Dewey

Timeline

Margaret Owings's Life		Historical Context
	1909	Archie Carr born
	1910	Jacques Cousteau born
Born April 29	1913	John Muir loses battle for Hetch Hetchy
	1914	John Muir dies
	1919	T. Roosevelt, conservation president, dies
Falls in love with the ocean	1922	Eugenie Clark born
	1930	Worldwide depression begins
Earns bachelor's degree, Mills Col.	1934	Beebe descends half mile in bathysphere
	1935	Sylvia Earle and Roger Payne born
	1936	David Suzuki born
	1940	Wangari Maathai born
	1948	Aldo Leopold dies
	1962	Beebe dies; Cuban missile crisis
Serves as commissioner of CA State Parks	1963	Pres. Kennedy assassinated
	1966	Tierney Thys born
Establishes Friends of the Sea Otter	1968	R.F. Kennedy, M.L. King Jr. assassinated
Serves as a trustee, Defenders of Wildlife	1972	Marine Mammals Protection Act passed
Receives Conservation Award, Interior Dept.	1975	Microsoft founded
	1979	Sylvia Earle dives deep in Jim suit
Blocks supertanker terminal site	1980	Arctic Wilderness gains protection
	1982	Richard St. Barbe Baker dies
Given Audubon's Dist. Service Medal	1983	Pres. Reagan proposes "star wars" defense
Husband Nathaniel dies	1984	Apple introduces Macintosh computer
Chairs Mountain Lion Preservation Fdn.	1987	Archie Carr dies
Receives UN's Environmental Gold Medal	1988	CDs outsell vinyl phonograph records
Given Sierra Club Dist. Service Award	1991	Soviet Union collapses
	1997	Jacques Cousteau dies
Voices from the Sea published	1998	International space station constructed
Dies at home, January 21	1999	Euro the new European currency

Earth Heroes: Champions of the Ocean

Eugenie Clark

1922–

The Shark Lady

*"Yes, it's true there are dangers. But
let's not exaggerate them. Instead, let's
define the limits of such dangers—even
if it doesn't make the most spectacular
account of one's experiences."*

It was Saturday morning at the New York Aquarium. A girl pushed open the door and paused to stomp the snow off her boots. The guards smiled. The girl was a regular. She had been coming every Saturday for weeks, ever since first visiting with her mother.

The guards had no idea that the girl would grow up to become one of the world's greatest *ichthyologists*—scientists who study fish. How could they? This was New York during the Great Depression. Back then, women rarely became scientists.

But this girl was very different. Not only would she become famous for studying fish, and especially sharks, she would also change the way people thought about scientists.

Eugenie Clark was born May 4, 1922, to parents who loved the water. Her father, Charles, owned a swimming pool. Her mother Yumiko taught swimming there. They were both skilled swimmers. But one day, Charles Clark went for a swim in the ocean and didn't return. Genie never knew her father.

Despite losing her husband to the ocean, Yumiko Clark was determined that Genie would not fear the water. She taught her little girl to swim even before she could walk. For her part, Genie watched her mother swim gracefully, as if she had been born in the sea.

Genie's mother was Japanese, here dressed in traditional attire.

But after Charles's death Yumiko had to give up teaching swimming, and worked full-time to support them at a job at a newsstand in Manhattan. During the day, little Genie stayed with her grandparents at their home in New Jersey.

In 1928, Genie, Yumiko, and her grandmother moved to Queens, one of New York City's boroughs. She was the only Japanese American child at her school, and sometimes her classmates were surprised by the traditional Japanese foods Genie's family ate and the customs they followed. Yet despite the differences, Genie made lasting friendships. She also skipped two grades!

On Saturdays, Genie traveled to the newsstand with her mother, and sat quietly while her mother worked. After her shift, Yumiko would take her daughter to lunch, and afterwards they might go to a movie or the zoo. But one day they went to the New York Aquarium, which until 1941 was located at Battery Park at the tip of Manhattan. Everything else paled in comparison. After the first visit, Genie wanted to go every Saturday. Eventually, she convinced her mother to drop her off at the aquarium, so she could spend the entire day there instead of at the newsstand.

At the aquarium, Genie pictured herself exploring the ocean floor. At the time, SCUBA tanks had not yet been invented; divers wore heavy suits and a helmet that covered the entire head. The diver's helpers pumped air through long hoses attached to the helmet. Although these diving suits were awkward and provided only limited movement, they allowed the first forays into the ocean lasting longer than the time a person could hold her breath. To be under the ocean and face to face with its creatures! Genie imagined herself walking along the sea bottom, with curious fish peeking into her diving helmet.

Genie was not alone at the aquarium; it was a place of refuge for homeless men forced to live on the streets during the Great Depression. Many people did not have jobs, and those who did had to be frugal with what little money they had. The men enjoyed listening to the nine-year-old expert, and they nicknamed her "Teacher." There was one problem with her days at the aquarium. Genie had to go home at the end of the day. The Saturday visits were all too brief.

Despite difficult economic circumstances, Genie asked for a fish tank for Christmas. Most parents at the time would have said no, considering a fish tank to be a luxury. However, Yumiko didn't think so. She realized that her daughter's interest in fish was serious and sincere—especially when Genie offered for her mother to consider the fishes as future birthday and Christmas presents! That Christmas, the Clark home installed the first of many fish tanks.

Genie spent hours observing her fish and taking notes on what she saw. Even though she had bargained away enough presents for several years, once in a while her mother came home from work with a new resident for the collection. Tanks filled the Clark apartment, and some land animals joined the collection, too—snakes, salamanders, and toads.

When Genie decided to study fish for a living, her mother and grandmother gently tried to discourage her. At the time, few women worked outside of traditionally "female" jobs, such as teacher, nurse, and secretary. They tried to persuade her to learn typing and shorthand. Perhaps, they suggested, she could become the *secretary* for a famous ichthyologist.

Genie would not be dissuaded. She entered Hunter College at age sixteen to study zoology. Part of her studies involved dissecting animal specimens. By studying dead creatures, she learned how their bodies were structured and how they worked.

As far as her mother and grandmother were concerned, dead animals belonged strictly in the college lab, not at home—but Genie sometimes let her scientific curiosity spill into the family kitchen. She once stored a dead monkey in the refrigerator, which upset her grandmother.

But the rat was worse. Genie got a dead rat from a local grocer, and took it home to clean the skeleton. To do so, she put the rat in a large pot, filled it with water, and put it on the stove. Genie thought she'd be able to get the rat boiled down before her grandmother returned home. Suddenly, Grandma was standing in the doorway of the kitchen. Curious about what Genie was cooking, she lifted the pot lid and . . . well, Genie was banished from the kitchen for quite a while after that.

Genie did well in school and in 1942 graduated from Hunter College with a bachelor's degree in zoology. The United States had

For her first published scientific paper, Genie studied a group of fish that included the pufferfish.

entered World War II in December 1941. No ichthyology jobs were available, and most jobs were aimed at supporting the war effort. Genie found a job working in chemistry. It wasn't ichthyology, but it paid well.

After work, Genie headed for night classes at New York University. One of her professors was Charles M. Breder, Jr., the former director of the aquarium where she had spent so much time as a girl. At his suggestion, Genie began studying the plectognaths, a group of fish that includes the cowfish, pufferfish, filefish, triggerfish, and the enormous ocean sunfish. They became the subject of her first published scientific paper, on which Dr. Breder listed her as co-author—a huge achievement for a twenty-five year old woman.

After the war ended, Genie received an important opportunity. Dr. Carl Hubbs of the Scripps Institution of Oceanography, which is part of the University of California, offered her a job as a research assistant and the opportunity to work toward a doctorate degree. Genie left New York and headed for Southern California.

During her time at Scripps, Genie's dreams became reality. She got the chance to walk on the ocean bottom in a diving suit, just as she had imagined years earlier while standing in front of the tanks at the aquarium in New York. "I was on the ladder, lowering myself into the cold water while the weight of the helmet flattened the goose bumps on my shoulders," she wrote of the beginning of the dive. Next, she found herself in an amazing world below the waves. The fish did not seem afraid of her at all, peeking in the window of the clumsy helmet with bright black eyes.

After some minutes enjoying the beauty around her, Genie realized she was having trouble breathing. She turned the helmet valve to let in more fresh air; it helped, but only briefly. Soon she was gasping for air. She staggered across the sea bottom toward the diving boat's anchor and the life line, her legs rubbery and thoughts slow from lack of oxygen. She reached the life line and gave it one long pull before she collapsed to her knees. As she fell, she realized that help would not come because a single pull was the signal for "I'm OK."

Her fall shifted the bulky helmet, and water rushed inside. "It was cool and refreshing and knocked some sense into my stupid head," she wrote. She removed the helmet and let her natural buoyancy take her back up toward the surface. As she surfaced, she saw "a shower of men" jump off the boat and come toward her. Dr. Hubbs reached her first.

After she recovered, she told what had happened — how she had opened the valve but to no avail. One man smirked, "Just like a girl to screw the valve the wrong way and cut off her air." But Genie had done everything right. The air hose, which had been mended recently, had leaked. Genie wasn't getting enough air! Despite the close call, she was determined to continue. She dived again before the day ended, and many, many times thereafter.

Genie returned to New York to work at the American Museum of Natural History. There she was a research assistant to Professor Myron Gordon, who provided her with a problem that she turned into a doctoral thesis: why was it that two species of fish that never crossbred in the wild would regularly crossbreed when in captivity—and produce offspring that were vulnerable to cancer?

To answer the question, Genie spent hours in the museum's hot and humid ichthyology laboratory, observing the fish. She learned that the females of both species preferred to mate with males of their own species. In the wild, same-species mates were easy to find, but in captivity, finding a mate was more difficult. So the females mated with males of a different species.

As Genie neared the end of her three-year project, she was presented with an exciting opportunity to do research in an exotic location: the islands of the South Pacific. At the time, little was known about the fish of the South Seas reefs aside from hearsay and fish stories. Genie could clear up many misunderstandings about which fish were poisonous and which weren't.

Genie told of her adventures in the South Pacific and the Red Sea in her fascinating book,
Lady with a Spear.

On the South Pacific trip, Genie collected and preserved thousands of specimens. But she also learned about people. She relied on local fishermen to help her locate the best diving sites to get good specimens. She could communicate with people who spoke Japanese or English; for others, she relied on hand signals. Yet without fail, they were friendly and helpful to this young American woman scientist.

The year 1950 was momentous for Genie. First, she received her doctorate, which freed her to choose her own areas of research. Second, she was awarded a Fulbright fellowship that would allow her to visit Egypt and study the creatures of the Red Sea. Third, she fell in love with a young physician named Ilias Papakonstantinou. While other men were resentful of Genie's interest in her career, Ilias found it fascinating. Genie and Ilias were married in New York before Genie left for a year to study the fish of the Red Sea.

She went to Egypt's Ghardaqa Marine Biological Station, which included labs, a museum, and a library. Some days she spent collecting specimens, then worked well into the night identifying and preserving them. "Often . . . only the thought of an early morning sailboat trip to another coral reef, where we might spend hours of strenuous diving, could force me to close the books in time for a decent night's sleep." The Red Sea would always be one of her favorite places to dive.

At the beginning of 1951, Genie returned to the United States, settling in Buffalo, New York, where Ilias had established a medical practice. Genie had her first child, Hera, in 1952. During the cold, snowy Buffalo winter, Genie began writing about her experiences in the South Seas. These writings became the book *Lady with a Spear*, published in 1953. A memoir of her early career, the book sold well and would change the direction of Genie's life.

Among the people who read *Lady with a Spear* were Anne and William Vanderbilt, members of a wealthy family. They invited Genie to visit their Florida estate. They wanted to set up a marine laboratory, and wanted her to run it. Six months later, Genie opened the doors of the brand-new Cape Haze Marine Laboratory in Placida, Florida. Soon after, Genie's second daughter, Aya, was born.

At the lab, a local fisherman named Beryl Chadwick became Genie's assistant. He knew the local waters and fish intimately. When sharks were needed for research, Chadwick knew how to catch them. Chadwick and Genie built a large pen for the sharks.

The big fish intrigued Genie—they always had, from the time of her childhood visits to the aquarium. Now she could investigate them freely in her own lab. At the time, sharks were thought to be mindless machines that lived only to kill. Yet Genie knew otherwise; she had seen sharks on many of her dives, and knew that a shark wouldn't attack without reason. She knew there was more to these fish than just teeth and hunger. So at Cape Haze, Genie conducted experiments to learn more about them.

The first experiment, which she planned with Dr. Lester Aronson, a noted animal behaviorist, sought to answer the question: Could sharks, which were generally perceived as stupid, learn to complete a simple task, pressing their snouts on a target to get a food reward?

Genie prepared a white wooden square for the target and placed it in a tank with two lemon sharks. At first, Genie and her team hung the food right in front of the target, so the sharks would learn to associate the white square with food. Then, the scientists moved the food away from the target. When a shark bumped the target, a bell rang. When the bell rang, the sharks were rewarded with food. It took time, but both sharks learned to press the square and ring the bell when they wanted food.

To make sure the results weren't a fluke, Genie changed the rules. Now, the shark was rewarded with food only when it pressed the square and then swam to a different part of the tank. They did it! Genie and her colleagues had proved that sharks could be taught.

During this exciting time, Genie and Ilias welcomed

Genie discovered that sharks are not eating machines, but have the ability to learn. Here she measures one.

Eugenie Clark

two more children into their family: Themistokles (nicknamed "Tak") and Nikolas (called "Niki"). But amid the joy, tragedy struck: Genie's mother passed away. Genie wrote, "I lost much interest in my work, felt I could no longer handle a full-time job, and thought that I should stay home with the children and help my stepfather." She closed the lab briefly, but after about six months, Genie went back to work. She moved the lab to its new location, Siesta Key, not far from her home.

Genie ran the Cape Haze lab for 12 years, and remains involved with it to this day, although it has a new name—the Mote Marine Laboratory—and a new location, Sarasota, Florida. Its mission is still the same as when Genie founded it: to learn more about the ocean and to share this knowledge with the public.

Genie left Cape Haze in 1967, following her divorce from Ilias. She went to New York and Maryland where she taught thousands of students biology courses ranging from "Life in the Oceans" and "Ichthyology" to "Sea Monsters and Deep Sea Sharks." Some of her classes had nearly 200 students enrolled!

Soon Genie found another fascinating phenomenon to investigate: the "sleeping" sharks of Mexico, the Caribbean reef shark. Although their eyes followed the divers as they swam around the cave, the sharks did not move. At that time, it was thought that sharks had to swim constantly to keep oxygenated water flowing over their gills, because, unlike bony fish, they cannot pump water over their gills. Here they were, holding perfectly still, yet clearly they were alive. Normally, when disturbed, a shark would swim away to settle in a new place, but these sharks could be handled and touched, and did not react. Why?

Eugenie wrote an article for *National Geographic* magazine about the phenomenon, and visited sites where sleeping sharks were found, off the coast of Japan and in the Red Sea. The sharks still haven't given up their secret to science!

Besides the sleeping sharks, Genie studied and swam with whale sharks, the largest of all the fish in the ocean, reaching lengths of fifty feet or more—nearly as long as a tractor-trailer. She also observed great white sharks from inside a steel cage—with the sharks circling outside.

And in the deep sea, she saw other kinds of sharks that were largely unknown to science. When she was diving in the deep-sea submersible *Pisces*, the sub was rocked by a shove from the outside. "It was nudged from below by a creature of enormous strength," Genie wrote. "Then this huge broad head came from underneath the sub. And the green eye of a shark was looking in as if looking at me." The curious visitor was a sixgill shark, a shark that lives in the lightless zone of the ocean below 1,500 feet.

One of Genie's most intriguing study subjects was a newly discovered species of shark named "megamouth." Genie dissected one of the few specimens of this unusual animal, and discovered not only that the female produces a number of eggs that mature inside her body, but also that the first baby shark that hatches eats the others inside the womb.

Genie's work with sharks led her to an unusual discovery. She proved that a Red Sea flat fish, the Moses sole, produces a natural and very effective toxin that repels sharks. Genie named the fish's toxin

Genie tried to unravel the mystery of the "sleeping" sharks. Sharks were thought to have to swim constantly to stay alive.

Eugenie Clark

"pardaxin." Since that discovery, other scientists investigated the possibility of using pardaxin to make a commercial shark repellant, but the chemical proved to be unstable unless freeze-dried. Although it won't work for human divers, it still works for the Moses sole.

During her time in Egypt in the 1950s and 1960s, Genie spent hours diving at a beautiful coral reef in the Red Sea called Ras Mohammed. The reef was full of colorful sea fans, an astonishing variety of coral formations, and other reef creatures from tiny clown fish to sleek sharks. Approximately 1,000 species of fish live in Ras Mohammed, as do 220 species of corals and 150 species of crustaceans.

In 1972, Eugenie published an article in *National Geographic* about one of the area's most unusual creatures, the "garden eels," long, slender fish that live with their tails in the sand, looking much like stalks of grass. When startled, the garden eels vanish backward into their burrows. Genie took her children with her as she tried to capture one of the shy creatures. They floated at the surface and watched. No luck. Suddenly, Genie realized her daughter Hera was splashing to get her attention: a garden eel was nearby and out of its burrow! Thanks to Hera's sharp eyes and Genie's quick reflexes, Genie got her specimen.

Because of its location, Ras Mohammed changed hands several times. After the Sinai War in 1967, it became part of Israel, and was protected. Later, it became part of Egypt, and fishing resumed. Some fishermen used dynamite, which killed hundreds of fish and destroyed the corals. Visitors to the area left trash behind and the reef began to look like a garbage dump.

Genie was not going to let Ras Mohammed be destroyed. She appealed to Egyptian President Anwar el Sadat. "I met him in person in Cairo. He gave me two cars that personally escorted me across the Sinai to Sharm el Sheikh," Genie recalls. "President Sadat was surprised to learn that the Sinai Peninsula had what I considered the most beautiful coral reefs in the world. He told me he would declare these reefs the first National Park of Egypt, but he was assassinated shortly before we were

Earth Heroes: Champions of the Ocean

to have the ceremony." Without Sadat's support, it seemed that Ras Mohammed might never be protected.

Then Genie heard that a fishing tournament was scheduled to take place on the reef. The tournament would wreak havoc on the reef; not only would the anglers go after the fish mercilessly, but boat anchors would destroy the corals. The tournament had to be stopped! Genie raced to the tournament's opening party, and marched right in, despite curious looks from the well-dressed guests. She found the man in charge of the tournament and told him that the tournament would damage the reefs terribly. Fortunately, the man knew of her work with Sadat. He agreed to move the tournament to a less-sensitive area.

Finally, in 1983, Ras Mohammed became Egypt's first national park. It was the first time any nation had made a marine site its first national park.

In 2008, Eugenie Clark received the Explorers Club Medal. Explorers Club president Daniel A. Bennett said, "These medals are given to those who make a lifetime contribution. This year, our theme was 'Exploring Planet Ocean.' With Genie's knowledge of sharks and her research, she was far and away the most qualified."

While exploring our planet and learning about its creatures, the Shark Lady has also taught human beings a few important things about the part we play in life on the ocean planet. 🍃

Fast Facts

Born: May 4, 1922, in New York

Husband: Ilias Papakonstantinou (divorced)

Children: Hera, Aya, Tak, and Niki

ACCOMPLISHMENTS:

- Proved that sharks could learn
- Among first to study the megamouth shark
- Studied the fish and reef life of the Red Sea
- Discovered pardaxin, a natural toxin and shark repellant
- Taught thousands of college students
- Responsible for the establishment of Egypt's first marine national park
- Led or served as chief scientist on more than 36 biological field programs
- Has four species of fish named after her
- Received the John Stoneman Marine Environmental Award (1982)
- Received the Medal of Excellence from the American Society of Oceanographers (1994)
- Presented with the Distinguished Fellow Award from the American Elasmobranch Society (1999)

RIPPLES OF INFLUENCE:

Famous People Who Influenced Eugenie Clark
William Beebe

Famous People Influenced by Eugenie Clark
Tierney Thys

TIMELINE OF IMPORTANT EVENTS

Eugenie Clark's Life

Historical Context

Eugenie Clark's Life		Historical Context
Born May 4	1922	Mussolini marches on Rome
Moves to Queens, NY	1928	Bubble gum, penicillin invented
	1930	Worldwide depression begins
	1934	Beebe descends half mile in bathysphere
	1935	Sylvia Earle and Roger Payne born
Earns bachelor's degree, Hunter Col.	1942	World War II fought
Earns master's degree in zoology, NYU	1946	"Iron Curtain" falls around USSR
Earns doctorate, zoology; wins Fulbright	1950	Sen. McCarthy on communist witch hunt
Publishes *Lady with a Spear*	1953	DNA discovered
Establishes Cape Haze Marine Lab.	1955	Civil rights movement intensifies
	1956	Iain Kerr born
	1962	Beebe dies; Cuban missile crisis
	1966	Tierney Thys born; Vietnam war fought
Joins faculty, Univ. of Maryland	1968	R.F. Kennedy, M.L. King, Jr. assassinated
Publishes *The Lady and the Sharks*	1969	Precursor of internet created
Writes *Nat'l. Geo.* article on garden eels	1972	Marine Mammal Protection Act passed
	1979	Sylvia Earle dives deep in Jim suit
Ras Mohammed made Egypt's first nat'l. park	1983	
First uses submersibles to study sharks	1985	
	1987	Archie Carr dies
Publishes *Desert Beneath the Sea*	1991	
	1997	Jacques Cousteau dies
Retires from Univ. of Maryland	1999	Margaret Wentworth Owings dies
Receives Explorers Club medal	2008	Obama first African-American president

Earth Heroes: Champions of the Ocean

Roger Payne

1935 – present

A Voice for Whales

"I thought if I studied whales, maybe I could find a way to change their fate."

In 1977 the people of Earth threw a message in a bottle out into space. The "bottle" was the spacecraft *Voyager*. The message was a gold-plated disk that carried the sounds of the planet. Most of the sounds were of human origin. There were words spoken in different languages, singing, and laughter. But the voice of another species was included on the disk: the songs of the humpback whale.

Just a few years before *Voyager's* launch, these songs had been recognized by biologist Roger Payne as a complex and hauntingly beautiful "language." And the whale songs had captured the imagination of the world.

Roger Payne was born January 29, 1935, in New York City. His father, Edward, was an engineer at Bell Telephone Laboratories. His mother, Elizabeth, played the viola and taught at the Mannes College Music School.

"Dad, because he was an engineer, was always a model for me," Roger recalls. Although he lacked his father's skill with physics, Roger, too, would enter the sciences. But first, his path traveled through New Jersey.

The family moved to New Jersey when Roger's father transferred to the Bell Lab located there. Their new home was in the country, and a stream ran through the yard. "I just thought I'd died and gone to heaven," Roger reminisces. The stream habitat was filled with living things, ready for a curious young mind.

In high school, his teachers encouraged his interest in biology. "I got interested in biology in high school when a teacher loaned me a book on birds," he says. The book opened his eyes to the possibilities of studying nature.

Roger decided to go to college and study biology.

Roger's interest in the sounds animals make was first piqued by his college experience with bat echolocation.

He was accepted to Harvard. At the time, Roger recalls, he "had no idea you could make a living doing something like biology." Then he was asked to baby-sit some bats, flying mammals that were the research subjects of Professor Donald R. Griffin. Griffin had discovered animal echolocation, the ability to navigate by producing sounds and listening for their echoes. Bats can avoid obstacles and catch prey even on the darkest nights, thanks to echolocation. Roger studied with Griffin and received his bachelor's degree in 1957.

He found the subject fascinating enough to continue with graduate school at Cornell University. There he turned his attention from mammals to birds, particularly the barn owl. He wrote his Ph.D. dissertation on how owls find their prey by listening for the small sounds the prey animals make. In 1962 he received his doctorate, and then as a postdoctoral fellow at Tufts University expanded his research to moths.

But something was missing. "I felt that what I was doing was not relevant to the problems that assailed the world around me. The wild world that I loved above all else was being destroyed."

Then Griffin, his former professor, asked Roger to work with him. Griffin was now at Rockefeller University in New York City, a graduate school and research center. In 1966, Roger left his position as an assistant professor at Tufts and went to Rockefeller to serve as an assistant professor and research zoologist at the university's Institute for Research in Animal Behavior, run in conjunction with the New York Zoological Society. Roger would remain at Rockefeller for the next 22 years.

At the time, the late 1960s, commercial whale hunters operated with little restriction in the world's seas, slaughtering thousands of whales each year and driving many species to the edge of extinction. People still thought of whales as big, vicious brutes, as they had been portrayed for many years in books and movies. "I thought, if I studied whales, maybe I could find a way to change their fate," Roger states.

Then he "lucked out like crazy." In 1967, he was invited to meet a man in Bermuda who worked for the U.S. Navy named Frank Watlington. Watlington was listening through hydrophones (underwater microphones) for Russian subs. Every once in a while, he heard something else, something he couldn't identify.

Roger and fellow researcher Scott McVay listened to the recordings Watlington had made of the mysterious sounds. They realized that the sounds were made by whales—and that they were amazing. The sounds covered a range of eight octaves, from high flutelike notes to deep rumbles. And they repeated after 15 minutes. They realized that the sounds were songs.

"We began listening and I thought, 'My God, these animals are repeating themselves,' and it was the most beautiful thing I'd ever heard from the wild world."

Although computers were not available at the time, they used a device to create "pictures" of the sounds on paper. The repetitive structure of the whales' sounds was clear.

"Back then, whaling was killing 33,000 whales a year, and it occurred to me that if we could get the music of the humpback whales into the ears of the world, we could stop the slaughter." In 1970 he released a recording of the whale music, called *Songs of the Humpback Whales*.

The whales were a hit. Roger and Scott's research was featured on the cover of *Science* magazine, the official publication of the American Association for the Advancement of Science (AAAS). Human musicians incorporated the whale songs into their compositions. The haunting voices became an anthem for the movement to stop whaling and protect the environment. *Songs of the Humpback Whale* is the best selling natural history recording of all time.

The public began to realize that whales were far from monsters. Rather, they were amazing creatures that were little understood—and also were in danger of being wiped out by human hunting. Although he didn't coin the phrase "Save the whales," Roger's work had a great deal to do with starting the movement. Along with the work of others such as Margaret Wentworth Owing's campaign on behalf of the sea otter, Roger's work contributed significantly to the passage of the Marine Mammal Protection Act of 1972. The oceans adjacent to U.S. coasts, at least, would be a "safe zone" for whales.

In 1976 an issue of *National Geographic* included a plastic record of whale songs. At 10.6 million copies, it is the largest single print order in the music industry's history, beating out Elvis and the Beatles.

Roger realized that the sounds made by humpback whales were not only hauntingly beautiful, but were the means by which whales communicated over thousands of miles.

Earth Heroes: Champions of the Ocean

Roger developed several theories about the vocalizations of whales. First, he theorized that the songs were a means of communication among the whales. Second, he thought that whales were able to communicate over very long distances—across oceans—using sound, because water transmits sound waves extraordinarily well. Roger wrote in his book *Among Whales*:

> In 1971 Douglas Webb and I calculated that before ship traffic noise permeated the oceans, fin whale blips [sounds] could have traved as far as four thousand miles and still be heard against the normal background noise of the sea. And on a quiet day in the pre-ship-propeller oceans they would only have fallen to the level of background noise after traveling thirteen thousand miles!

Research now shows that whale sounds can carry through water up to 1,850 miles.

However, not everyone was enamored with Roger's work. At the time, human beings were believed to be the only living things that could think, reason, and communicate. The idea of a whale using sound to communicate over long distances in the ocean and even singing a song—and changing that song over time—flew in the face of this belief that many people held dear.

The result? A backlash. Some scientists ridiculed Roger's theories. "When it first came out it very near ruined my career to suggest that whales could hear each other across oceans," he recalls. The disrespect of his colleagues made it increasingly difficult for him to obtain grants. Yet he persisted.

He also revolutionized whale research. He proved to his colleagues that it was not necessary to kill a whale or any other creature in order to study it, contrary to the practice that had gone on for hundreds of years.

Roger did not stop there. He and his wife, Katy, also a biologist, decided to go to Argentina to learn more about whales. They and their four children camped on the Argentine coast to observe the migrations of the southern right whales.

One day, Roger came upon a female whale dozing in the shallows near the family's camp.

> After a while she opened her eye and looked me all over. You could see her eyeball rolling in her head—the eyes move very well—and then she closed her eye again. Basically, the whale was just saying, 'Well, if you seen one of these, you've seen them all.' And I thought, 'Oh, that's the greatest compliment I've ever been paid by a whale.'

What also struck him was the fact that the whale—a member of a species renowned for its supposedly aggressive behavior toward humans—hadn't responded at all to his presence. In a *National Geographic* article, Roger wrote, "During that first season, we discovered extraordinary evidence of right whales' restraint toward humans."

Roger's study of the southern right whale has continued since 1970. During that time, he developed the method now used by whale researchers around the world, identifying whales by the unique markings on their bodies. Roger has identified more than 1300 individual whales while studying their movements, migrations, social structure and behavior, and population recovery.

It was on a beach in Argentina that Roger met a young man who would become not only vital to Roger's work but also a noted conservationist himself: Iain Kerr. Iain had been born in Scotland in 1956. His family lived in the United States before settling in the village of Lostwithiel, Cornwall, England. Each day when school was not in session, his parents would "throw me out the door in the morning and I'd come back at night." He spent the time exploring, following his curiosity and developing a healthy respect for the land around the village. Before long, it would turn into a respect for the power of the sea and an enduring admiration and concern for its creatures.

Although trained as a teacher, Iain followed his own path, founding a company that built hovercraft and then making a living sailing. Among the people he met while being a "sail bum" was one of the founders of Greenpeace, John Paul Govin, who invited him to go on an expedition to Argentina. "And it was there on a beach in Argentina that I met Roger Payne."

He had no idea who Payne was at the time. All he knew was that Payne was going looking for whales, and that he needed a boat captain. Iain quickly signed on. The two have worked closely ever since. Their work has taken them around the world by land, sea, and air—the latter often by commercial airplanes, but sometimes in more interesting aircraft, as in the photo below.

In 1971 Roger established a two-part non-profit organization: the Whale Conservation Institute to promote research and education, and the Ocean Alliance, to advise educators and policy makers. Today, Roger serves as the president of Ocean Alliance and Iain is the chief executive officer. As part of his Ocean Alliance work Roger has worked tirelessly to

Roger (left) and Iain used this ultralight plane for filming Discovery Channel's "In the Company of Whales" and for observing large groups of whales.

defend whales against slaughter, through public appearances, lectures, and newspaper and magazine reviews. He has helped people understand that whales are not the monsters as they had been portrayed, but instead are intelligent, complex beings who live in societies much like our own.

In 1986, Roger's efforts bore fruit when the International Whaling Commission put in place a moratorium on whaling. In countries around the world, people pressured their national governments to support the whaling ban. For Roger, Iain, and all the others who had pushed for the moratorium, it was a reason to celebrate.

Unfortunately, whaling continues. Japan claims to hunt whales for scientific purposes, although the meat ends up in grocery stores. Norway and Iceland simply ignore the Commission's rules about whaling. And around the world, pirate whalers stalk their prey. More work remains to be done.

Although whaling had wreaked havoc on the world's whale populations, Roger realized that pollution is an even greater threat. He wrote in *National Geographic*, "Pollution will soon replace the harpoon as the next mortal threat to whales and, ultimately, humanity."

Pollutants don't stay where they are produced. As Iain says, "Whatever you drop on the ground ends up in the ocean. Gravity never sleeps." Even though it may take years, pollutants on the land and in the air find their way into the sea—and into the bodies of the creatures that live there.

A look at the marine food pyramid explains a lot. At the base are millions upon millions of plankton organisms, each one taking in minute amounts of pollutants that have entered the sea. The plankton are eaten by krill, small shrimp-like creatures. The krill, in turn, are eaten by mackerel. Typically the mackerel get eaten by bigger fish, like cod, and the cod are eaten by tuna. The tuna end up eaten by a shark, and the shark gets eaten by a sperm whale. The process by which every particle of pollution consumed by every creature in the food chain ends up in the top predator is what scientists call *bioamplification*.

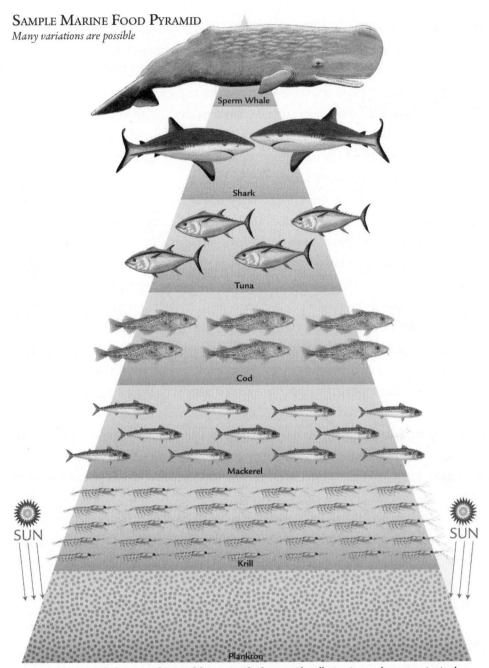

SAMPLE MARINE FOOD PYRAMID
Many variations are possible

Sperm Whale

Shark

Tuna

Cod

Mackerel

SUN

SUN

Krill

Plankton

Because sperm whales are at the top of the marine food pyramid, pollution ingested at any point in the pyramid is eventually concentrated in the bodies of the whales. The process is known as bioamplification.

Roger, Iain, and the team from Ocean Alliance began to study ocean pollution by studying whales. Roger wanted to collect tissue samples from sperm whales and test them for evidence of pollution. Because it is the most massive predator in the sea, the sperm whale was an ideal choice for this experiment. How many pollutants are present in their bodies? What are they? How are they affecting the whales? "No one knows how polluted the oceans are because no systematic, global study has been made," explains Iain.

To answer those questions, they devised the five-year, round-the-world research journey called the "Voyage of the *Odyssey*." They made plans to sail the organization's 93-foot sailing ship, the *Odyssey*, to the equatorial Pacific, where many female sperm whales spend most of the year. Male sperm whales join them for mating season, arriving from places impossible to reach with a ship and bringing with them valuable information about pollution loads in far-flung areas.

And although Roger and Iain only proposed to take a single skin sample the size of a pencil eraser from each whale, the first obstacle for the project was obtaining permission to study the whales at all. Sperm whales are protected globally. They cannot be hunted or harassed. Getting permission for the study required dozens of permits that had to be chased down and then presented at the appropriate times during the journey. That job fell to Iain, who now knows more than he ever imagined about the bureaucracies of many countries.

The law protects endangered species from harm, and also prohibits the import or export of their hides, tusks, horns, bones, or other body parts. But the law does not distinguish between a tiger skin intended for decorating the floor of a penthouse and whale tissue for a scientific study meant to protect the whales themselves, as well as people.

Because of the potential delays involved with the complexity of the bureaucracy in every nation the *Odyssey* sailed through, there was concern about what would happen to the samples once they were collected. The plan was to take the cells from the whales and grow them in a special

In 1971 Roger founded the Ocean Alliance, which operates the Odyssey, *a research sailing ship. As in this photo, Roger often peers from the bowsprit for whales.*

environment called a culture; by growing additional cells, the samples available for testing would be larger. "The sooner you get the cells into a culture, the better the chances are of saving the cells and growing the cell line," Iain explains. Because of several close calls in which the precious samples nearly spoiled because of delays, they decided to install a full-fledged cell-line laboratory in the *Odyssey,* something unheard of on a sea vessel.

But how do you get a whale to give a tissue sample? You have to be quick and a good shot with an arrow. All hands on the *Odyssey* kept their eyes open for signs of a sperm whale's spout, or "blow." Each species of whale produces a unique pattern when it exhales, and so the crew could recognize a sperm whale at a distance. Then the *Odyssey* would head for the whales, trying to get there before the whales sounded, or dove, again.

Roger under the bowsprit of the Odyssey. *Pollution is replacing the harpoon as the greatest threat to whales, he says.*

Each time, Roger was the first person to clamber out onto the *Odyssey's* bowsprit, despite having two artificial knees. There he dangled dangerously high over the water, but also got the best view. Meanwhile, another crew member took careful aim with a crossbow and fired. If the arrow struck the whale, its tip cut out a sample of skin and blubber no bigger than a pencil eraser, but valuable beyond measure. The arrow got scooped up with a net and its precious cargo collected for the lab. The whale, meanwhile, went onward, as though nothing had happened.

In the lab, the samples collected from the whales could be preserved quickly. They could also be increased in size using special cell-growth media, allowing many tests to be run, even though the original sample was quite small. The crew of the *Odyssey* worked with experts at the Woods Hole Oceanographic Institute in Massachusetts, one of the world's oldest and most respected marine research organizations.

Earth Heroes: Champions of the Ocean

As the data collected over the five-year voyage began to be analyzed, something disturbing was found. Every sample contained evidence of contamination. In particular, Roger's team found DDT and polychlorinated biphenyls (PCBs). These are suspected cancer-causing chemicals developed in the 1930s and not produced since the 1980s.

"It's sobering to discover that these toxicants are distributed globally, although how dangerous a threat they pose at low concentrations is not yet known," says Roger. He wants to make people aware of the unknown dangers posed by ocean pollution. "Seafood is the principal source of protein for over a billion people. You could easily argue that this is the largest public health crisis in the world."

In addition to his scientific research on humpbacks, southern right whales, and now sperm whales, Roger has also increased public awareness of the whales through books and films. His work has been featured in more than 30 television documentaries, including the Emmy award-winning *In the Company of Whales* (1991). He co-wrote and co-directed the IMAX film *Whales* (1998). He has written two books, including *Among Whales*, published in 1995, and many magazine articles.

Working in concert with the International Whaling Commission, Roger and Iain have helped several countries set up marine sanctuaries, safe places for whales and for the entire habitat. In 2008, Papua New Guinea established a 1.25-million-square-mile marine mammal sanctuary, largely because of Iain. In recognition of his efforts regarding pollution, Iain received the Chevron Conservation Award in 2006.

In addition, Roger and his second wife, actress Lisa Harrow, perform a two-person show called *SeaChange: Reversing the Tide*. Through such diverse voices as Shakespeare, Robert Frost, and Wendell Berry, they make the case that human beings are not above nature, but rather are an integral part of it, and that survival depends on paying attention to nature's laws.

The Whale Conservation Institute and Ocean Alliance conduct educational outreach programs around the world. In fact, students and

Roger, Iain, and a booby enjoy a sunset from the Odyssey's *bowsprit. Roger says that saving the world requires a change of mind.*

teachers were able to follow the *Odyssey's* voyage via the Internet on the PBS and Ocean Alliance web sites.

Roger has been recognized by a wide variety of organizations. In 1978 he was made a knight in the Order of the Golden Ark for his work in conservation by Prince Bernhard of the Netherlands. In 1984, he received a MacArthur Foundation "genius grant," an award of $250,000 for the recipient to use as he or she sees fit. The United Nations Environmental Program named him one of the "Global 500" leaders of world conservation. He also received the Joseph Wood Krutch Medal in Conservation from the Humane Society of the United States. In 2007 Oxford University presented him with the Dawkins Prize for Animal Conservation. In 2008 he was a finalist for the Indianapolis Prize, the largest individual monetary prize in the world for animal conservation, presented every two years by the Indianapolis Zoo. And the National Geographic Society has called him the "dean of whale research."

Yet Roger's work is far from complete. The whales are still threatened. Besides the threat of pollution, they are being hunted by several nations, including Japan. On the Ocean Alliance website, Roger wrote an open letter to the young people of Japan, urging them to protest their nation's killing of whales, especially the humpbacks, whom he called "composer/singer/poets." He describes the creativity of humpback whales and points out how great a loss the death of a single whale can be to the species' music.

> So although the fishery only kills a few humpbacks each year it wouldn't have had to kill very many to destroy these greatest of known singers. After all, the man who shot John Lennon only killed one man in his life, but what an appalling loss.

Together, Roger Payne and Iain Kerr are working to prevent the potential disaster of widespread human illness caused by eating poisoned fish. Roger hopes that perhaps one day we will be able to say that we not only saved the whales, but that we were saved by the whales, as well. In his book *Among Whales*, Roger wrote:

> What I am saying is . . . conservation is simply a state of mind. That all we have to do to save the world is to change how we view the importance of the wild world. Saving the world is not a job that requires some highly developed technology, or some arcane new science, or some hitherto undeveloped social system. It requires that simplest of things—changing our minds . . . It is not some other person's responsibility, but ours . . . This is the challenge of the future—what we must accomplish if we are to save ourselves and some significant fragment of life on Earth.

Fast Facts

Born: January 29, 1935, New York City

Wife: Katherine Payne (divorced); Lisa Harrow

Children: John, Holly, Laura, and Sam

ACCOMPLISHMENTS:

● Discovered that humpback whales communicate with songs

● Discovered that whales communicate over long distances

● Studied the effects of pollution on whales

● Has studied every species of large whale

● Studied the southern right whale in the longest continuous study of a baleen whale

● Developed many techniques used by whale researchers, including using photographs to identify whales by their physical markings

Famous People Who Influenced Roger Payne
Donald Griffin, Thom Eisner, E.O. Wilson, Carl Sagan

Famous People Influenced by Roger Payne
Peter Tyack, Hal Whitehead, Jim Darling, Chris Clark—and, as Roger says, "one never knows."

Timeline

Roger Payne's Life		Historical Context
	1934	Beebe descends half mile in bathysphere
Born January 25	1935	Sylvia Earle born
	1941	U.S. enters World War II
Receives bachelor's degree from Harvard	1957	Russia launches first satellite, Sputnik
	1956	Iain Kerr born
Receives doctorate from Cornell	1962	Beebe dies; Cuban missile crisis
	1966	Tierney Thys born
Begins studying whales	1967	Several civil rights riots in U.S. cities
	1968	Owings founds Friends of the Sea Otter
Songs of the Humpback Whales released	1970	Students killed at Kent State Vietnam protest
Founds Ocean Alliance & Whale Cons. Inst.	1971	U.S. voting age lowered from 21 to 18
	1972	Marine Mammal Protection Act passed
	1973	Cousteau Society established
Nat'l Geographic inserts whale song record	1976	U.S. celebrates bicentennial
Knighted by Netherlands' Prince Bernhard	1978	Apple computer founded in a garage
Declares pollution a major threat to whales	1979	Sylvia Earle dives deep wearing the Jim suit
Receives MacArthur Fdn. "genius grant"	1984	Apple releases Macintosh computer
	1987	Archie Carr dies
	1997	Jacques Cousteau dies
Begins *Voyage of the Odyssey*	1999	Margaret Wentworth Owings dies
Receives Dawkins Prize, Animal Conservation	2007	Gore gets Nobel Peace Prize on climate
Is a finalist for the Indianapolis Prize	2008	Obama elected first African-Amer. president

Earth Heroes: Champions of the Ocean

Sylvia Earle

1935–

Her Deepness

"The greatest era of exploration of this ocean planet has just begun!"

The first time Sylvia went to the beach, a large wave reared up and knocked her over. Other little children might run back to their parents, crying and begging to go home. Sylvia did no such thing. She picked herself up and chased the wave back out to sea!

It was a prophetic first encounter. It was as if the sea could not wait to introduce itself to the person who would unravel some of its mysteries. And it was as if little Sylvia could hardly wait, either. One day, like an "ocean astronaut" tethered to a yellow submarine, she would walk in a special suit on the ocean floor, in a dive that was far deeper than any other human of her time.

Sylvia Alice Reade Earle was born on August 30, 1935, in Gibbstown, New Jersey, and grew up on a small farm. Her parents, Lewis and Alice, both loved the outdoors. They encouraged their daughter's love of nature and allowed her to roam freely in the woods around the farm. "I wasn't shown frogs with the attitude of *yuck*," Sylvia recalled. "But rather, my mother would show my brothers and me how beautiful they are and how fascinating it was to look in their gorgeous golden eyes."

When Sylvia was twelve, the family moved to Florida's Gulf Coast. For many young people, leaving their old home and friends is a difficult experience, one laced with sadness and loss. There was some of that for Sylvia, who loved her home in New Jersey. But at the family's new home, the Gulf of Mexico—one of the world's most biologically rich bodies of water—came right up to her backyard. Sylvia got to meet some fascinating new neighbors, like the bottlenose dolphins. "I longed to swim with their grace and speed," she later wrote. She watched how they breathed through the blowhole, actually a nostril on the tops of their heads. She admired how they could see just as well above water as below it.

As a teenager, Sylvia eagerly learned to use a snorkel and mask so she could visit the animals of the Gulf in their own world.

Her parents encouraged her love of biology, but also, as a precaution, urged her to get her teaching credentials and learn how to type, "just in case." However, as Sylvia recalls, her ninth-grade science teacher, Edna Turnur, "encouraged, rather than stomped on, my exceptional interest in science and natural history as a *girl*—at a time when girls were supposed to be focused on home economics and the arts."

The family did not have much money, but Sylvia was an excellent student, and after high school she decided to go to college and study biology. After completing junior college, she won scholarships that paid for her tuition at Florida State University. There she met Harold Humm, a professor who taught a graduate class in marine biology. He let her take his class although she was only an undergraduate, and he eventually became one of her greatest supporters.

In Professor Humm's class, Sylvia learned to use a SCUBA tank, which in the summer of 1953 was still a relatively new invention.

> With my first breath I swallowed a little salt water, but I could get air even though my head and body were completely submerged. I adjusted my bite on the mouthpiece, took a second breath, then another, and soon forgot about breathing because it was so easy, and concentrated on looking at a small yellowish brown fish—a grunt—that clearly was looking at me.

For Sylvia, these first forays into the grunt's world were the beginning of a career studying the ocean and diving ever deeper below

Sylvia admired the grace and speed of the bottlenose dolphin, and with SCUBA gear could finally swim with them.

the waves. "In my mind, I had been transformed irreversibly into a sea creature who henceforth would spend part of the time above water."

After earning her bachelor's degree in biology in 1955, Sylvia moved to North Carolina to attend Duke University, where Humm served as advisor for her master's and doctorate studies. Yet she never truly left the Gulf of Mexico. Because every master's candidate must do a research project, Sylvia decided to study the algae in the Gulf. Algae are plants or plantlike organisms that live in water. They can be as tiny as a single cell or as huge as a forty-foot-tall piece of kelp. Since the late 1950s, she has collected more than 20,000 specimens.

Sylvia did not realize at the time just how useful her school research project would become decades later. She says, "When I began making collections in the Gulf, it was a very different body of water than it is now—the habitats have changed. So I have a very interesting baseline." A baseline is a sample, or set of samples, that a scientist uses in making comparisons with other samples. She was awarded her master's degree in botany in 1956.

During her time at Duke, she met her first husband, John Taylor. Soon after they were married, she said, "my new husband almost immediately was swept away aboard a ship to the Mediterranean, and was gone for several months. I had an opportunity to go to work, and get to see real fish, not fish in a book." She worked for the U.S. Fish and Wildlife Service for a while, and then she, John, and their two children moved to Florida. Sylvia enrolled at the University of Florida at Gainesville.

> Once again, I took a job in the same department where I was taking classes. It certainly helped financially, but I think even more, it helped put my feet solidly on the ground, becoming tuned into what the real professionals were doing. . . . They accepted me as part of their team, not just as a student.

In 1964, upon Humm's recommendation, she was offered a botanist's position on a six-week expedition to the Indian Ocean, sponsored by the National Science Foundation. They were going to dive in places where no one had dived before. "I was the only woman among 70 men, but Humm seemed confident that that would not be a problem—and it wasn't. The only problem that developed for me was an incurable passion for exploring unknown parts of the ocean."

She returned to Duke and her former professors, and in 1966 earned her doctorate degree. And that master's degree research project that she had started ten years earlier? She kept building on it. She made a lifelong project of cataloging every species of plant that lives in the Gulf of Mexico.

In 1968, Sylvia had her first experience riding in a submersible, an undersea craft designed for research and exploration. The *Deep Diver* took her only 100 feet down, but it was enough to excite her imagination at the possibilities.

After briefly serving as the resident director of the Cape Haze Marine Lab in Florida (which had been founded by Eugenie Clark), Sylvia moved north to Massachusetts. There, she took on two jobs: one as a research fellow at Harvard University's Farlow Herbarium, the other as a research scholar at Radcliffe College, which at the time was the women's college of Harvard.

During her time in Massachusetts, she learned about an exciting experiment. Is it possible for people to live and work underwater for extended periods of time? To answer that question, the United States government established the Tektite Project, a research facility on the sea bottom where scientists would live 24 hours a day for weeks at time. Sylvia applied to take part in the project. She was turned down, not because she wasn't qualified—she had thousands of hours of underwater experience—but because the project leaders were uncomfortable with the idea of men and women living and working together!

Fortunately, the following year Tektite II was undertaken with all women scientists. Sylvia and four other female scientists lived and worked for two weeks in the facility. After diving at extreme depths, a diver normally must spend time in a decompression chamber to help the

Sylvia shows a specimen to a fellow aquanaut inside Tektite II, their underwater "home" and research lab.

body readjust to surface pressure. While living on Tektite II, this was unnecessary. Instead, the scientists could come and go as they pleased. They lived on the ocean floor 24 hours a day!

"Imagine washing the dishes . . . then stepping through a round hole in the floor and swimming off into the sea," she said. Sylvia and her fellow researchers observed fish at all hours and learned more about their behavior than ever before. "I discovered that fish, like people, have food preferences. Some damselfish even establish and maintain gardens of the plants they like to eat!"

When the Tektite II scientists emerged, they discovered that they were famous. Sylvia was in demand as a public speaker. *National Geographic* asked her to write an article about the experience.

> My first reaction was an emphatic NO, but I changed my mind after coincidentally reading comments by a British scientist, Thomas Huxley, written a century earlier, who admitted that fellow scientists might look down upon those who communicated scientific findings to the public at large, but that he believed it to be an obligation, a way to give back to those who supported the research in the first place. He also cautioned, though, that scientists have an obligation not to stretch the truth to make a better story, the truth always being the best story of all. Fantasy is fine if labeled as such, and there is a place for science fiction but not masquerading as the truth.

Her articles for *National Geographic* about the ocean world were well received. Through speeches and lectures, and books written for children and adults, she began telling people about the need to protect the ocean and its creatures.

Sylvia was one of the first researchers to use the self-contained underwater breathing apparatus (SCUBA), which Jacques Cousteau and Émile Gagnan had invented. But " diving has its limits.

At the surface, the layer of the Earth's air above us presses down on our bodies at 14.7 pounds per square inch, known as one *atmosphere*. The human body is built to withstand this pressure, so it feels normal. But being under a layer of water is a completely different thing. At just 33 feet below the water's surface, the body is under pressure equal to two atmospheres, or 29.4 pounds per square inch. Every 33 feet down, the pressure of another atmosphere is added. The human body simply can't withstand the great pressure and cold of the deep ocean.

But that didn't stop Sylvia. She heard about the "Jim Suit," which was created to inspect oil platforms for damage. The suit is like a hybrid of a suit of armor and a diving bell. "These atmospheric diving suits resemble a walking refrigerator, or the Michelin Man, or a big white bear with joints," Sylvia explained.

The idea behind the Jim Suits—named for the first person willing to wear one, Jim Jarrett—is to provide access to deep water but avoid the need for decompression. Sylvia wondered if the Jim Suit could be used to explore the deep sea, and convinced its developers to let her use it and see how deep she could dive.

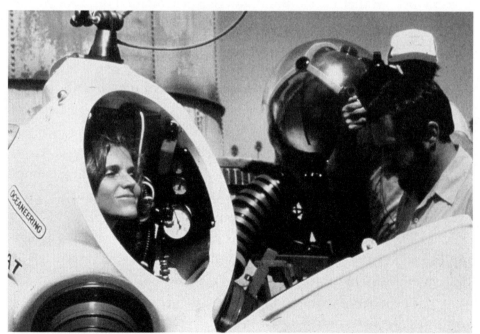

Sylvia prepares for her historic dive 1,250 feet below the surface in an astronaut-like device, the Jim Suit.

On September 19, 1979, Sylvia climbed into the bulky Jim Suit. She stood on a platform attached to the front of the *Star II*, a bright yellow submarine owned by the University of Hawaii and operated by Maui Divers. As the *Star II* descended through the sunlight zone of the ocean into the darkness, it took Sylvia with it. Down and down the sub went, until it landed with a thump on the sea floor, 1,250 feet down. Sylvia detached herself from the sub's platform and began walking around. Only a thick black communications cable attached her to the *Star II*. "It's the only time that this atmospheric diving suit, or any of the atmospheric diving suits, have been used in this way. Typically, they do have the cable going back up to the surface."

Encased in the protective titanium Jim Suit, Sylvia was walking where no human being had ever walked before. Later she told Peggy Orenstein for the *New York Times Magazine*, "When I got to the bottom, I stepped off and walked on the ocean floor for two and a half hours. It was a nice parallel: that's about how long [astronauts] Buzz Aldrin and Neil Armstrong were on the moon. It took them longer to get there, of course, and it cost more. But I had the fun of seeing all kinds of critters out there."

Like the astronauts, Sylvia brought her environment with her. The suit kept her warm, provided her with oxygen, and protected her from the weight of 37 atmospheres that bore down on every square inch. She could walk around and touch things with the suit's mechanical hands. She could also pull her hands out of the Jim Suit's arms and write notes about what she saw, including an 18-inch-long shark with glowing green eyes, bright red crabs clinging to a pink sea fan, and "sparks of living light, blue green flashes of small transparent creatures brushing against my faceplate." It reminded her of William Beebe's description of his descent in the bathysphere in *Half Mile Down*, which she had read as a kid.

Her experience with the Jim Suit made her wonder: was it possible to go still deeper?

Sylvia expressed her desire to dive even deeper to Graham Hawkes, an English engineer who had helped design the Jim Suit. Together, on the back of a napkin, they sketched out plans for a deep-diving submersible. To bankroll the craft, Sylvia and Hawkes started their own companies, Deep Ocean Engineering and Deep Ocean Technology. In 1984, that sketch became a reality, a vehicle named *Deep Rover*.

Deep Rover owed a debt to the bathysphere before it. Like the bathysphere, it was a sphere, but rather than being made of cast metal, its sphere was made from five inches of clear plastic that provided the diver an unobstructed view in all directions. "It looks like a little submarine, but it is, in fact, a diving suit," she explained. However, unlike vehicles such as the *Alvin*, it was a one-person device meant to be operated by a scientist. "The idea has always been that scientists couldn't be trusted to drive a submersible by themselves because they'd get so involved in their work they'd run into things."

Deep Rover reached 3,000 feet off the coast of California—a little more than a half mile down. Once again deep in the world of darkness, Sylvia saw animals that make their own light. She saw fish with glowing pockets below their eyes that they could flick shut when approached by one of the fearsome deep-sea predators. She saw strange jellyfish and sea stars, sea cucumbers tiptoeing along on pseudopod feet, and tripod fish standing on the seafloor on long spines extending from their fins.

She saw something glittering and red too, and it made her curious. Most animals of the deep sea are dark or colorless; red is a color only seen in the upper levels of the ocean. When *Deep Rover* reached the red object, she realized with dismay that it was a soda can! "It was not really a surprise," she wrote in her book, *Dive!*

> Whatever gets tossed into the sea doesn't just go away; it settles down
> in some other place, out of sight but not really gone. Some bits of junk
> are quietly being transformed into a home for sponges and small fish,
> like miniature shipwrecks in the sea, but I felt like apologizing on

"I felt like apologizing" for human debris landing among deep species like the tripod fish, brittle starfish, and the sea pig cucumber.

behalf of my species for raining debris on the unsuspecting communities of life in the deep.

In 1990 Sylvia became the chief scientist of the government agency responsible for ocean exploration, the National Oceanic and Atmospheric Administration (NOAA). Part of NOAA's job is to encourage ocean exploration and conservation, while taking into account the needs of fishermen, crabbers, lobstermen, and others who make their living by catching and selling sea creatures. Sylvia, however, does not eat sea creatures, and is opposed to ocean fishing. She didn't get along very well with some people, so left the position after a year and a half.

She began to work on "Ocean Everest," another deep sea project. Just as Mount Everest, at 29,035 feet above sea level, is the highest point on the land, this project's goal was to explore some of the lowest points on the planet's surface. Her collaborators on the Ocean Everest project were Japanese scientists. They developed a piloted submarine called the *Shinkai 6500*, which in 1989 dove to the amazing depth of over four miles: 21,409 feet, or about 6,500 meters.

But Sylvia wanted to explore even further, and in 1995, she succeeded. The *Keiko*, a remote-operated vehicle (ROV), dove into the Challenger Deep, part of an undersea trench in the Pacific Ocean near Japan. Reaching a depth of 36,008 feet, Keiko nearly reached the lowest point on Earth's surface.

Sylvia shared her experiences with the public through books and films. She has made films about coelacanths, humpback whales, and kelp forests. Her books for adults and children include *Sea Change, A Message of the Oceans*; *Dive! My Adventures in the Deep Frontier*; *Wild Ocean*; and *Hello, Fish! Visiting the Coral Reef*.

In 2009 she received a unique opportunity: she was named the winner of a TED Prize. TED stands for "Technology, Entertainment, Design," a conference that brings together leaders in computer technology, entertainment, and communications. The TED Prize is $100,000 in cash plus unparalleled access to other TED leaders who can help fulfill the winner's wish. What did Sylvia wish for? She made a wish for the ocean, of course:

> I wish you would use all means at your disposal—films! expeditions! the web! more!—to ignite public support for a global network of marine protected areas, hope spots large enough to save and restore the ocean, the blue heart of the planet.

Sylvia's work has had impact beyond education. After reading her book *Sea Change*, Ed Harte, a former newspaper publisher, was inspired to establish a research center concentrating on the Gulf of Mexico. Today, Sylvia is an advisor to the Harte Research Institute for Gulf of Mexico Studies at Texas A&M University at Corpus Christi.

Since 1999, Sylvia has been one of the National Geographic Society's Explorers-in-Residence. The Society not only publishes a famous magazine, it is also an organization dedicated to learning and exploring. As an Explorer-in-Residence, Sylvia is encouraged to keep learning more about the deep sea and the amazing animals that live there. As part of her work with the National Geographic Society, Sylvia led the Sustainable Seas Project, a cooperative effort between the National Geographic and NOAA. The project's goal was to survey the United States' marine sanctuaries, which are safe havens for marine life like national parks are for animals on land.

Sylvia, shown here in the Deep Worker, *has spent more than 6,000 hours underwater and holds the depth record (over 3,200 feet) for solo diving.*

Using the next generation of submersible, *Deep Worker,* the participants in the Sustainable Seas Project found a greater diversity of life in the sanctuaries than they had expected. Analysis of the data gathered over five years will provide an unprecedented picture of life in the oceans.

Sylvia has received many awards and accolades, recognizing both her achievements as a woman and her conservation efforts. In 2004, Earthwatch Institute presented her with its Conservation Award. In 2005, the Girl Scouts of America gave her its Powerful Woman Award. She's also been presented with many honorary degrees and named to numerous halls of fame, including the National Women's Hall of Fame.

Sylvia's entry and subsequent honorary presidency of the Explorers Club is particularly satisfying. This famous club was established in 1904 and includes many of the world's most eminent explorers—people like Robert Peary (first to the North Pole), Theodore Roosevelt, and John Glenn (first in space). However, the Explorers Club didn't admit women to its ranks until 1981, when Sylvia and three other women were accepted. In 2000, she was elected the club's honorary President.

In 2000 the Library of Congress presented her with its Living Legend Medal. Sylvia has been given several nicknames including "Defender of the Deep," "Guru of the Deep Blue," and, of course, "Her Deepness."

Sylvia's influence now reaches everyone through "Google Ocean." In 2006, she met John Hanke, Maps Director of Google Earth. She thanked him for making Google Earth, a wonderful way to view our planet. Then she challenged him. "But, John, when are you going to finish it? You should call Google Earth, 'Google Dirt.' What about the three-quarters of the planet that is blue?"

Hanke admitted that she was right. "We on the Google Earth team had been working hard to build a rich 3D map of the world, but we had largely ignored the oceans—two thirds of the planet. Inspired by Sylvia, the team got to work." As a result of Sylvia's prodding, Google installed a map of the ocean floor in Google Earth, so a viewer can now drop below the ocean surface and explore the nooks and crannies of the ocean floor.

Sylvia is known for the remarkable rapport she develops almost instantly with fish when she swims with them. Perhaps the key to this connection lies in her words:

> As a biologist, there are two things that I have come to see as the most wondrous aspects of living creatures. One is that no two are alike. It isn't just that there are no two human beings—but that in itself is remarkable enough. . . . Mosquitoes look alike to us, but there are no two that are identical. Every fish is different. . . . The other part is the flip side of it: the common ground that all life has. We see basic physiological processes repeated time and time again. . . . We are all together in this, we are all together in this single living ecosystem called planet earth. 🍃

Fast Facts

Born: August 30, 1935, Gibbstown, New Jersey

Husband: John Taylor (divorced); Graham Hawkes

Children: Elizabeth and John

ACCOMPLISHMENTS:

- One of the first four women elected to membership of the Explorers Club
- Dove to 1,250 feet in the Jim Suit
- Co-designed *Deep Rover* and other submersibles
- Named an Explorer-in-Residence by the National Geographic Society
- Named a Living Legend by the Library of Congress
- Received the TED Award
- Encouraged the development of Google Ocean

RIPPLES OF INFLUENCE:

Famous People Who Influenced Sylvia Earle
Howard Humm, William Beebe, Lewis R. Earle, Alice R. Earle, Katherine Bowen, Edna Turnur

Famous People Influenced by Sylvia Earle
Tierney Thys

Timeline

Sylvia Earle's Life		Historical Context
	1934	Beebe descends half mile in bathysphere
Born August 30	1935	Roger Payne born
Moves to Florida's Gulf Coast	1947	Marshall Plan assists post-war Europe
Learns to use SCUBA equipment	1953	DNA discovered
Earns bachelor's degree, Florida State Univ.	1955	Civil rights movement intensifies
Earns master's degree, Duke Univ.	1956	Iain Kerr born
	1962	Beebe dies; Cuban missile crisis
Earns doctorate from Duke Univ.	1966	Tierney Thys born; Vietnam war escalates
Takes first dive in a submersible	1968	R.F. Kennedy, M.L. King Jr. assassinated
Takes part in Tektite II	1970	*Songs of the Humpback Whales* released
	1972	Marine Mammal Protection Act passed
Dives to 1,250 feet in Jim Suit	1979	Sony introduces Walkman
Co-designs *Deep Rover* submersible	1984	PG-13 movie rating created
	1987	Archie Carr dies
Becomes chief scientist at NOAA	1990	Hubble telescope launched
Keiko ROV dives to 36,008 feet	1995	Oklahoma City Federal Bldg. bombed
	1997	Jacques Cousteau dies
Leads Sustainable Seas Expedition	1998	Named Nat'l Geog. Explorer-in-Residence
	1999	Margaret Wentworth Owings dies
Named Library of Congress's Living Legend	2000	Human genome deciphered
Receives TED Award	2009	Google introduces Google Ocean

Earth Heroes: Champions of the Ocean

Tierney Thys

1966 – present

Unraveling the Mystery of the Ocean Sunfish

"You have to put yourself in the animal's place."

When Tierney Thys was little, you couldn't buy a child-sized wet suit. Tierney's father loved to surf, and the Thys family spent a lot of time in the ocean. But the big Pacific waves tossed Tierney and her three sisters around, and the cold water chilled them to the bone. "The Central Pacific Coast is not a particularly kid-friendly ocean," Tierney recalls.

Tierney's mom and dad wanted their children to be able to enjoy the ocean, too, so they decided to make wet suits for their daughters. As a resourceful engineer, Tierney's dad found some neoprene fabric and glued it into little suits. Tierney's mother decorated the rubbery fabric with nail-polish flowers. The suits worked. They kept the girls warm in the water.

But there was one catch. Dad hadn't installed any zippers. The fabric was stretchy and difficult to get out of. "I lost gobs of hair whenever we took them off," Tierney says. So the wet suit went on in the morning and stayed on all day. It was kind of a dress rehearsal.

Although today Tierney is a marine scientist using computer technology to learn about one of the ocean's largest fish, she often still dons a wet suit and dives in.

Tierney Thys was born December 31, 1966, in San Leandro, California. She was the youngest child of Thierry and Barbara Thys. "I've always had a passion for studying biology, and particularly animal

form and function," she says. "Even when I was just six years old, I loved to page through my older sister's high school biology text and find diagrams exposing the inner workings of living creatures."

As a child, she spent lots of time outdoors, especially in the waters of the Pacific. "If you are interested in animal diversity, the ocean's the place to be," she says. The little girl loved the ocean and the many animals she saw there. She became interested in how their bodies reflect what they do. "Some animals really give away how they work—you look at a shark or a tuna and you can tell that it's all

Tierney's dad made wet suits for his daughters before they could be purchased in children's sizes.

about speed and strength. You can see that they're predators."

When Tierney was ten years old, her parents separated and she left California with her mom and moved to Vermont, the only state in the Northeast that doesn't have a seacoast. "I missed the ocean," she recalls. Although there was a beautiful stream on the property where they lived, it just wasn't the same. When she was 15, she learned to SCUBA dive in a Vermont lake. But her time at the beach had left its mark. Her love for the ocean "was a welling-up inside me that I couldn't suppress."

She decided to go to college and study marine biology. After graduating from Brown University in Rhode Island, she went to visit her father in California. His casting foundry happened to be near a company called Deep Ocean Engineering, which happened to be run by the explorer Sylvia Earle and her then husband, Graham Hawkes.

Delighted to meet the famed explorer and fascinated by the company's projects, "I started hanging around," Tierney says. After working at Deep Ocean as a volunteer, Tierney was hired, and worked there from 1989 to 1991. There she met another employee, Brett Hobson. Brett and Tierney were married in August 1997.

At Deep Ocean, the young scientist became good friends with the famed explorer. Recognizing a sharp mind and an adventurous spirit when she saw it, Sylvia encouraged Tierney to go to graduate school. Sylvia wrote a recommendation for Tierney and urged her to apply to Duke University in North Carolina, the same university that Sylvia had attended for her doctorate. Tierney was accepted, and in 1998 graduated with her doctorate degree in zoology.

It was during her graduate studies at Duke that Tierney discovered the creature that would captivate her for years to come: the ocean sunfish.

> I first became enchanted with the ocean sunfish after seeing a tiny picture of one on my graduate school advisor's wall. To me it just seemed such an unlikely design for any self-respecting open ocean fish. It completely piqued my curiosity and has held me spellbound ever since.

The ocean sunfish, of which there are three species, is among the ocean's most unusual-looking fish. Its scientific name, *Mola*, means "millstone," a reference to its disk-shaped body. Ocean sunfish are huge: they often weigh more than 500 pounds. From the top and bottom of the ocean sunfish's body protrude large dorsal and anal fins. The distance from the tip of one to the tip of the other averages about 10 feet. The largest specimens on record have measured 14 feet from fin tip to fin tip, 10 feet long, and more than 5,000 pounds.

Most curious, though, is the ocean sunfish's lack of a tail. Instead of a tail, its body ends in a peculiar little "rudder." The rudder is actually made up of rays from the dorsal and anal fin that "migrate" rearwards while the fish grows. This migration of body parts occurs rather the same way that a baby flounder has an eye on each side of its body, but as it ages, one eye moves across the fish's head so that both eyes end up on the same side.

Ocean sunfish hold the record for the most eggs produced at once by any *vertebrate* animal—one with a backbone. Although many fish produce thousands of eggs at a time, one four foot female ocean sunfish was found to be carrying an estimated 300 million eggs.

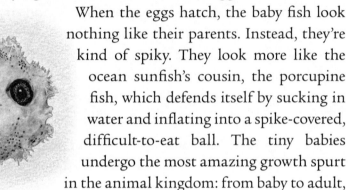

When the eggs hatch, the baby fish look nothing like their parents. Instead, they're kind of spiky. They look more like the ocean sunfish's cousin, the porcupine fish, which defends itself by sucking in water and inflating into a spike-covered, difficult-to-eat ball. The tiny babies undergo the most amazing growth spurt in the animal kingdom: from baby to adult, the ocean sunfish increases its weight 60 million times. "It's as if your little baby grew to the size of six *Titanics*," explains Tierney, referring to the huge ocean liner that sank in 1912.

These cute baby sunfish are the size of the tip of a pencil.

One would expect a big, round fish to have a powerful tail to propel it around. But instead, it has no tail at all. The ocean sunfish doesn't seem suited for moving fast. In fact, it hardly seems suited for moving much at all. "This is really a counter-intuitive design for an open ocean vehicle," Tierney says. Other open-ocean, or *pelagic* fish, are streamlined, such as the mako shark, the swordfish, and the bluefin tuna.

In fact, the ocean sunfish had a reputation for being one of the ocean's laziest residents. Most scientific articles stated that the fish were like enormous plankton, simply drifting along wherever the current took them. At sea, ocean sunfish were often found lying on the water's surface, soaking up the sun—thus the common name ocean sunfish—a behavior upon which their lazybones reputation was based.

Tierney wasn't ready to accept the conventional wisdom that the ocean sunfish was just a big, floppy, lazy fish. And she was right.

You have to "put yourself in the animal's place" to begin to understand it, she explains. A fish's place is extremely different from that of a human being.

Compared to fish, human beings live in an almost two-dimensional world. The Earth's surface is relatively flat. As victims of gravity, our natural state is not to go up and down very much. We're flatlanders.

Fish, on the other hand, swim in their watery world free from the usual constraints of gravity. They live fully in a three-dimensional world. They move up and down as

Its habit of sunbathing on its side gave the ocean sunfish its name—and its reputation as lazy.

readily as north, south, east, and west. It's hard for us, as flatlanders, to really comprehend what life is like in a world like that. The real story of the ocean sunfish, Tierney discovered, has three dimensions.

Tierney wanted to understand the ocean sunfish's story, and led a team of biologists to investigate. Yet finding ocean sunfish isn't easy. Unlike many fish species, once they reach adulthood they don't live in schools, but live alone in the vast open ocean. If it had not been for spotter planes and "spa treatments," finding one might have been like looking for the proverbial needle in a haystack. Fortunately, they had high-tech equipment to help.

In a small plane, a team member would fly over the ocean, watching for ocean sunfish resting at the surface. When one was spotted, the pilot would radio its coordinates (latitude and longitude) to the rest of the tagging team, which would head for the spot. Quietly they would sneak up on it, toss a net over it to keep it from diving, and then attach a high-tech satellite tag to the base of its dorsal fin. The team took care not to hurt the fish during the process. For its part, the ocean sunfish didn't seem to mind too much, being naturally easygoing. In fact, Tierney says, the ocean sunfish is the only fish you can swim up to and give a nice scratching.

And the spa treatments? Ocean sunfish love to be groomed. They gather around kelp patties, floating mats of a seaweed called kelp that are home to many smaller fish. There, the big fish assume a special position that tells the small fish in the kelp that the sunfish are not there to eat, but rather, that they want a treatment. The small fish swarm over the giant ocean sunfish and clean parasites from their thick hides. The ocean sunfish enter a trancelike state while being cleaned. They hold still and roll their eyes back in their heads. At that point, it's possible for a tagging-team member to swim up and attach a satellite tag.

This tagging gun was one of the methods Tierney used to attach a satellite tag to an ocean sunfish.

Earth Heroes: Champions of the Ocean

Fifty years earlier, Archie Carr attached metal ID tags to turtles in the hope that someone, somewhere, would find it, understand what it was saying, and notify him where it was found. Unlike Archie's simple ID tags, Tierney uses "pop-up archival satellite tags." They are computerized devices that record water temperature, depth, and time, and store the data over a pre-determined length of time. When that time is up—six months, a year, even two years—the tag pops off the fish and floats to the surface. Orbiting satellites overhead can receive its signals and upload the tag's recorded data. The satellites then transmit those data to the team's computers.

By studying the data from the 46 ocean sunfish archival satellite tags, Tierney has discovered that the big fish aren't "megaplankton" as so many believed. Instead, they spend their days diving, over and over, as many as 30 or 40 times, slowly propelled by the waving of their fins.

Many of the dives take them down to the ocean's "deep scattering layer." The deep scattering layer is a zone of the ocean that is full of living things. It rises to near the surface at night, and sinks downward during the day. Among the creatures found in the deep scattering layer are jellyfish, the ocean sunfish's primary prey.

The ocean sunfish, Tierney discovered, can dive to depths of nearly 2500 feet. There they presumably hunt for their prey in the dark. Then they rise near to the surface again, where it is thought the sunlit waters warm them up in preparation for another dive. The water temperature changes tremendously as they dive. Near the surface it may be 68 degrees F; deep down, it may be as cold as 34 degrees F.

The satellite tags also record light levels along with the time of midday. With these measurements and some additional calculations, researchers can figure out the north-south and east-west movements of the tags. Before Tierney's research, no one knew where these giant ocean sunfish went. Did they ride the currents from the California coast to Japan and back? Did they swim directly across the Pacific on a seasonal schedule? Did they go north in spring and south in the winter?

Tierney swims with this sunfish after attaching a satellite tag to the base of its dorsal fin. The tag will later pop off, float to the surface, and transmit its data to a satellite.

It turns out that ocean sunfish are homebodies with fairly well-established home ranges.

As she studied the ocean sunfish, Tierney became aware of a terrible problem facing these gentle giants: fishing. It's not that ocean sunfish are being caught and consumed in great numbers. In fact, they aren't typically eaten in North America and Europe because their meat, when cooked, is rather unpalatable and watery. So what's the problem? It's that the ocean sunfish are caught in nets meant for other species of fish. Scientists call these accidental victims "bycatch."

Although no longer used in some parts of the world, drift nets have been a common tool of fishermen. Made of nearly invisible monofilament line, these nets hang and can be as long as 55 miles. They capture creatures indiscriminately, from ocean sunfish and sharks to dolphins and whales. Drift nets are deadly curtains in the sea.

Off the California coast, ocean sunfish make up 26 percent of the total bycatch taken in drift nets. Among swordfish fishermen in the Mediterranean, the numbers are even worse. Ocean sunfish can make up a full 90 percent of the animals caught accidentally.

Bycatch causes the unnecessary death of hundreds, even thousands, of animals in each net drawn in. Ocean sunfish caught in the swordfish nets are thrown back into the sea, where many likely die from the injuries and stress of being netted. Off the coast of South Africa alone, an estimated thirty thousand ocean sunfish have been killed as bycatch over the past 10 years.

An additional consequence of bycatch of the ocean sunfish may be an unchecked growth in the jellyfish population. Remember that ocean sunfish are homebodies. If all the ocean sunfish from a certain area of the ocean are captured and die as bycatch, other ocean sunfish won't move in to replace them. That means that people have removed the top predator of jellyfish in the area. An ocean full of jellyfish is an ocean out of balance.

There is a need, Tierney says, to spread awareness of these remarkable animals and alert people to the perils of bycatch. We also need to examine the target fishery—the fish that the fishermen are trying to catch. Is it critical for human survival? If it is, what techniques can be used to reduce bycatch? "The ocean sunfish aren't the only victims," she explains. Sharks, rays, and many other fish species are caught as bycatch.

"The more you learn, the more you know that you don't know," Tierney says. For example, what physical adaptations have made ocean sunfish so well suited to their habitats? How is it that they grow so large on a diet of watery prey? Yet she can spread the knowledge she has gathered in an effort to protect the ocean sunfish from death by bycatch.

While researching the ocean sunfish, Tierney has followed in the footsteps of Beebe and Cousteau as well as John Muir and David Suzuki (see *Champions of the Wilderness*) by reaching out to the public and educating them about science. In 2001, as the science editor and then later Director of Research for the Sea Studios Foundation in Monterey, California, she helped produce the award-winning documentary series called *The Shape of Life*. Funded in part by the National Science Foundation, *The Shape of Life* told how animals came to be. "I love the fact that we were able to

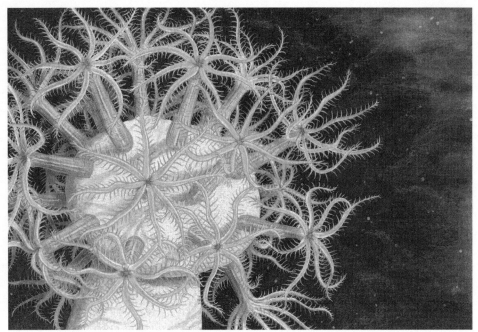

Tierney has been active in producing award-winning documentaries such as The Shape of Life, *featuring such important characters in evolution as corals, anemones and jellyfish. This is a mushroom coral.*

bring to the silver screen some of the more unsung but nonetheless spectacular and evolutionarily significant members of the animal world, for example, sponges, jellyfish, flatworms, echinoderms, and more."

She went on to another ambitious project with Sea Studios, the National Geographic's television series *Strange Days on Planet Earth.* "For this project, we dove into the inner workings of the planet to show how Earth operates as an integrated system and how our perturbations to the atmosphere and ocean can have far-reaching and at times counter-intuitive impacts," she explains. The series won top honors at the Wildscreen Festival in 2005 known as the "Green Oscars." Knowledge can be shared with huge audiences through television programs. *Strange Days* has been seen by more than 20 million people around the world.

Tierney notes that the advent of television and the Internet has changed how scientists work. Computer technology, such as that involved with the satellite tags, is constantly changing, with devices getting smaller and yet increasingly powerful at the same time. "It's a very exciting time to be in conservation biology," she says. "We have these tremendous resources available."

Tierney has proposed an intriguing possibility. What if the animals themselves became research vessels? Oceanographic equipment is prohibitively expensive, running hundreds of thousands of dollars, if not more. Getting time and funding to use submersibles like *Alvin* and *Johnson Sea-Link* is not easy. What if satellite tags on marine animals were used to collect data? What if reports from elephant seals could be used to study ocean currents and seawater oxygen levels along the California coast? What if blue whale diaries could be transmitted to measure the effects of climate change? What if hammerhead sharks could be used to find the secret places in the ocean where numerous large species gather—kind of like the marine equivalent of the watering holes of the Serengeti on land?

Some researchers have begun using tagged animals as research "assistants." When biologists, oceanographers and engineers work together, there is tremendous potential.

Unlike scientists working just 10 or 20 years ago, Tierney uses the Internet as a tool. Email brings her communications from colleagues all over the world who are working with her on the ocean sunfish project. Even social networking sites like Facebook and MySpace can be "massively progressive," she says. Her web site, www.oceansunfish.org, includes a page inviting citizen scientists to report the locations and circumstances of their own encounters with ocean sunfish. In response, she's heard from people around the world and of all persuasions—"Catholic nuns, Jewish rabbis, Muslims, Christians—and we're all united by our love of life," she notes.

The data from Tierney's ocean sunfish research are being incorporated into a larger effort to understand the ocean's top predators. The project, called Tagging of Pacific Predators, is part of the Census of Marine Life, a 10-year project to find out how diverse, widely distributed, and abundant marine life is. In addition to the ocean sunfish, the TOPP

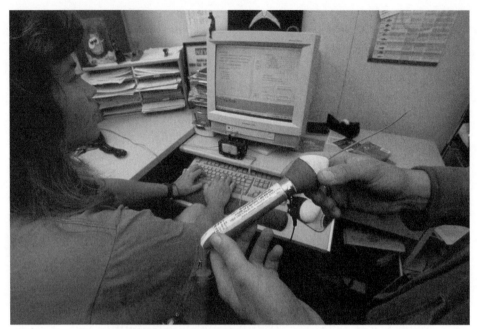

A high-tech satellite tag (in foreground) provides vastly more information to Tierney than could the old-style ID tags used by early researchers such as Archie Carr.

project is tracking some of the ocean's most charismatic animals, including the blue whale, great white shark, leatherback sea turtle, elephant seal, and black-footed albatross.

By gathering basic information about how these diverse species feed and breed, and relating it to data about ocean currents, temperature, and salinity, scientists can begin to understand how the ocean environment affects life in the sea.

This information will be vital to the ongoing effort to establish marine sanctuaries around the world. On land, vital habitats are set aside as national or state parks, which protect them from development, hunting, and other changes. Similarly, people are working to set aside areas of the ocean. Fishing, trawling, and collecting are tightly regulated in marine sanctuaries. These are areas that truly provide safe havens in the sea. "The marine sanctuaries can protect the ocean habitats, and by protecting habitats, we can better protect the variety of species that live there," Tierney says.

But while eleven percent of the world's land habitats are protected, less than one-tenth of one percent of the ocean has been protected in this way. "There are hundreds of marine protected areas, but most are quite small," Tierney explains. As of early 2009, the United States has 14 marine protected areas. Creating marine sanctuaries, or parks, takes a lot of effort. Convincing the public and the politicians that a sanctuary is needed is just one large step.

"Humans must start acting as a global species," Tierney says. People now sometimes plan 20 years into the future, but she says that we need to think farther ahead—and not just about our own community. She is pleased that her work has helped many people realize that they are part of "something so much bigger. What connects us also strengthens us."

The cost of research is high. For example, one satellite tag costs $3,500! Yet Tierney's work has attracted many supporters. In 2000 she received a grant from the Lindbergh Foundation, a nonprofit group that supports environmental research. In 2003 she received a Women in International Science Collaboration grant from the American Association for the Advancement of Science (AAAS). In 2004 National Geographic presented her with its "Emerging Explorer" award, which provided her with $10,000 to support her work.

Tierney Thys is in the vanguard of a new generation of marine scientists who are using technology not only to conduct research but also to spread knowledge. Like Eugenie Clark before her, she's helping change humanity's perception of an entire species. That is truly no small feat.

And yet, she says, "I never feel like I can really call myself a marine biologist. It's such a lofty title! There's so much to know—how can you possibly know everything there is to know?"

Fast Facts

Born: December 31, 1966, San Leandro, California

Husband: Brett Hobson

Children: Marina and Grant

ACCOMPLISHMENTS:

- Studied the ocean sunfish for more than a decade, shedding new light on this mysterious open-ocean fish

- Developed a web site that connected people from around the world to the research

- Worked with eBay to reduce the sale of invasive species over the Internet

- Was named a National Geographic Emerging Explorer

- Developed the award-winning television series, websites and outreach materials for National Geographic's *The Shape of Life* and *Strange Days On Planet Earth.*

- Member of the Census of Marine Life—the largest oceanographic project in history.

RIPPLES OF INFLUENCE:

Famous People Who Influenced Tierney Thys
Eugenie Clark, Sylvia Earle, Jacques Cousteau, Pablo Neruda, David Attenborough, and "Mr. Green Jeans" of the *Captain Kangaroo* TV series (1955-1984)

Famous People Influenced by Tierney Thys
you?

Timeline

Tierney Thys's Life		Historical Context
	1962	William Beebe dies
Born December 31	1966	Vietnam war fought
	1970	*Songs of the Humpback Whales* released
	1979	Sylvia Earle dives deep in Jim suit
	1987	Archie Carr dies
Receives bachelor's degree in biology	1988	NASA scientist warns of global warming
Meets Sylvia Earle, works for Deep Ocean	1989	Berlin Wall falls
Wins a Sigma Xi grant-in-aid	1995	Keiko ROV dives to 36,008 feet
	1997	Jacques Cousteau dies
Receives doctorate; works with Sea Studios	1998	
	1999	Margaret Wentworth Owings dies
Science editor, *The Shape of Life*	2000	Census of Marine Life launches
Director for *Strange Days On Planet Earth*	2001	NY World Trade Center destroyed
Joins Census of Marine Life tagging team	2001	Scientists warn of global warming
Featured speaker at TED conference	2003	
Named a National Geographic "Emerging Explorer"; launches oceansunfish.org	2004	Tsunami hits Asia after undersea earthquake
Becomes BeachComber for Monterey Bay marine sanctuary	2007	
Joins National Geographic expeditions to Baja, Galapagos, Antarctica and Alaska	2008	
Develops National Geographic children's TV conservation series	2009	Obama first African-American president

BECOME A HERO!

You've read about some pretty amazing people. They really are heroes. But you might be thinking, "I can't do something like that. I can't be a Tierney Thys or a Roger Payne or an Archie Carr."

Not true! When each of these Earth Heroes began—and even when they finished—they didn't see themselves as setting out to change the world. Remember that if the problems facing our world are great, then so must be the opportunities for change—and everything starts with one person's idea.

The men and women whose stories are told in this book have changed the way that we look at the oceans around us. Jacques Cousteau showed us the mysteries that lie beneath the waves. Eugenie Clark revealed that sharks are not mindless killing machines but creatures supremely adapted to their environment. Roger Payne shared with the world the magnificent singing of whales.

Their achievements may seem beyond the reach of mere mortals like you and me. We may never dive to record-breaking depths, discover previously unknown facts, or wind up saving a species from extinction (but then again, you may!). To be an Earth Hero, you don't have to do big things. Seemingly small things are heroic, too.

Remember Margaret Owings? She started small, working from her dining-room table to alert people to environmental threats. She wrote letters to newspapers and articles for magazines and spoke out against what she felt was wrong. Everyone can do that. You can write letters to newspapers and TV stations, call your government representatives, blog and Twitter about the things you feel strongly about. Stand your ground; there will always be those who jeer from the sidelines or stand in your way—and that's their right, too. Present the facts honestly (remember Sylvia Earle's advice!) and you'll be far ahead of them.

"I'm too shy," you may say. "I can't speak out like that." That's fine; not everyone needs to be a public activist. You can make a change in the privacy of your own home. Recycle; it sounds old-fashioned, but it makes a big difference. Reduce what you consume by choosing wisely when you shop; look for items with less packaging.

Consider how you and your family do everyday activities. Do you carry your lunch to school in a reusable container? Do you really need a new cell phone, or are you just going along with the advertisers who want you to think so?

The answers are different for everyone. There are thousands of small changes you can make. Each change probably won't seem to make much of a difference to the world as a whole. Just remember that one snowflake is small, but billions make an avalanche!

Today, more than ever before, you can help scientists learn about our planet. Through the Internet, scientists seek the help of citizen-scientists—people like you—who are curious about the world. With the help of dozens, hundreds, or even thousands of citizen-scientists, researchers are able to gather more data faster than ever before.

A perfect example of citizen-scientists in action is the annual Great Backyard Bird Count, run by the Cornell Laboratory of Ornithology. Each year, citizen-scientists around the country observe birds, make note of the species they see, and count individual birds. The results give the Cornell scientists a wonderful "snapshot" of the conditions of bird populations around the country. To learn more, including how you can take part, visit http://www.birds.cornell.edu/. Similarly, Tierney Thys asks citizen-scientists to report their sightings of ocean sunfish on her web site, www.oceansunfish.org.

The Internet connects scientists and the public. By using technology, you can learn about the planet and the work being done to protect it. However, be sure to read like a scientist: be a bit skeptical. Because the Internet is wide open, anyone can post anything. Read, think, find out about the writer's background, and in the end, make up your own mind.

Making choices and changes, even small ones, may take courage. The other customers at the supermarket may raise their eyebrows when they see you bring reusable bags to the store, but if you have courage, you'll prevent the use of paper or plastic. You might be more comfortable getting a ride to school from your parents, but if you have the courage to take the bus, you'll save fuel. And if you walk or take your bike, that's even better! Encourage your family to save up errands and do them at once, rather than making repeated trips.

Each person you've read about has changed our planet. You can make a change, too, if you are brave. I'll bet you are.

SOURCES AND CREDITS

Every effort has been made to obtain permission from the relevant copyright holders. If you have additional information please contact the publisher.

WILLIAM BEEBE

Beebe, William. *Half Mile Down* (New York: Harcourt Brace & Co., 1934).

Gould, Carol Grant. *The Remarkable Life of William Beebe: Explorer and Naturalist* (Washington, D.C.: Island Press, 2004).

Matsen, Brad. *Descent: The Heroic Discovery of the Abyss* (New York: Pantheon Books, 2005).

PHOTO CREDITS: p.8, 10, and 20, courtesy of Carol Grant Gould; p. 13, © Wildlife Conservation Society.

ARCHIE CARR

Carr, Archie. *A Naturalist in Florida: A Celebration of Eden* (New Haven, Conn.: Yale University Press, 1994); *Handbook of Turtles* (Ithaca, NY: Cornell University Press, 1952, 1995); *The Windward Road* (Tallahassee: The Florida State University Press, 1955, 1979).

Davis, Frederick Rowe. *The Man Who Saved Sea Turtles* (New York: Oxford University Press, 2007).

PHOTO CREDITS: p. 24, 27 and 36, courtesy of Mimi Carr; p. 33, courtesy of Dr. Jeanne A. Mortimer.

JACQUES COUSTEAU

Cousteau, Jacques, with Frederic Dumas. *The Silent World* (New York: Harper & Row, 1953).

Cousteau, Jacques, with Susan Schiefelbein. *The Human, the Orchid, and the Octopus* (New York: Bloomsbury, 2007).

Narins, Brigham, editor. *Notable Scientists from 1900 to the Present*, Volume I (Farmington Hills, Mich.: Gale Research, 2001).

PHOTO CREDITS: p. 44, courtesy of C.N. Pique; p. 47, courtesy of F. Charlet, Ocean Futures Society; p. 49 and 52, courtesy of Ken Pratt; p. 50, courtesy of B. Deguy, Ocean Futures Society.

MARGARET WENTWORTH OWINGS

Owings, Margaret Wentworth. *Voice from the Sea: Reflections on Wildlife and Wilderness* (Monterey, California: Monterey Bay Aquarium, 1998); *Artist, and Wildlife and Environmental Defender*, an oral history conducted by Suzanne Riess and Ann Lage, University of California Regional Oral History Office.

PHOTO CREDITS: p. 57, 63 and 64 photos by (respectively) William A. Garnett, Amyas and Evelyn Ames, and Ted Streshinsky, from Nathaniel Alexander Owings, *The Spaces In Between* (Boston: Houghton Mifflin, 1973); p. 66, courtesy of Sisse Brimberg, KEENPRESS; p. 68, courtesy of Nathaniel Alexander Owings and Jennifer Owings Dewey.

Eugenie Clark

Clark, Eugenie. *Lady with a Spear* (New York: Harper & Brothers, 1951, 1952, 1953).

McGovern, Ann. *Shark Lady: True Adventures of Eugenie Clark* (New York: Scholastic, 1978).

Ross, Michael Elshon. *Fish Watching with Eugenie Clark* (Minneapolis: Carolrhoda Books, 2000).

PHOTO CREDITS: p. 72, 79, and 84, courtesy of Eugenie Clark.

Roger Payne and Iain Kerr

Ocean Alliance web site: www.oceanalliance.org.

Author interviews with Roger Payne and Iain Kerr.

PHOTO CREDITS: p. 90, 96, and 98, courtesy of Iain Kerr Ocean Alliance; p. 93, 100, courtesy of John Atkinson Ocean Alliance; p. 102, courtesy of John Sherman, H-O Photographers.

Sylvia Earle

Earle, Sylvia. *Wild Ocean: America's Parks Under the Sea*, with Wolcott Henry (Washington, D.C.: National Geographic, 1999).

Earle, Sylvia. *Dive! My Adventures in the Deep Frontier* (New York: Scholastic, 1999).

Conley, Andrea. *Window on the Deep: The Adventures of Underwater Explorer Sylvia Earle* (Boston: New England Aquarium, 1991).

TED lecture: www.ted.com/index.php/talks/ sylvia_earle_s_ted_prize_wish_to_ protect_our_oceans.html

PHOTO CREDITS: p. 109 and 111, OAR / National Undersea Research Program (NURP); p. 115 and 118, courtesy of Harte Research Institute for Gulf of Mexico Studies.

Tierney Thys

Author interview with Tierney Thys.

TED lecture: www.ted.com/index.php/talks/ sylvia_earle_s_ ted_prize_wish_to_ protect_our_oceans.html

Ocean Sunfish web site: www.oceansunfish.org.

PHOTO CREDITS: page 122, courtesy Barbara Tierney; p. 125, 128, 132, and 134 courtesy of Mike Johnson, Earthwindow. com; p. 126, courtesy of Tim Rock, Doubleblue.com.

INDEX

Earth Heroes: Champions of the Ocean

ABOUT THE AUTHORS AND ILLUSTRATOR

Photo courtesy of Kathy Black

"Writing this book was a thrill for me, because so many of these people are my own heroes," says author Fran Hodgkins. She combined her love of the ocean and her ability to write and became a writer. She's written 20 books for young readers, most of them related to science, nature, or animals. A native of Massachusetts, she lives with her family and pets in Maine, not far from the sea.

Photo courtesy of Julie Stoessel

Cris Arbo was born on Martha's Vineyard Island, Massachusetts, and has lived by the sea much of her life. She received her degree in art and theater from William Paterson University. Her art has appeared in books, magazines, calendars, cards, murals, and in animated feature films, TV shows, and commercials. In addition to creating artwork, Cris has raised four daughters. She and her husband, author Joseph Patrick Anthony, live with their youngest daughter in central Virginia.

OTHER BOOKS FROM DAWN PUBLICATIONS

ALSO IN THE EARTH HEROES SERIES

Earth Heroes: Champions of the Wilderness (available now)
Earth Heroes: Champions of Wildlife (available Spring 2010)

OTHER BOOKS ABOUT NATURE AND GREAT NATURALISTS

Girls Who Looked Under Rocks by Jeannine Atkins, illustrated by Paula Conner. The six women portrayed were often discouraged from getting dirty, much less pursuing careers in science. Yet all grew up to become award-winning scientists and educators—frequently the only women in their fields.

John Muir: My Life with Nature by Joseph Cornell. This unique "auto-biography" of John Muir is told in his own words, brimming with his spirit.

How We Know What We Know About Our Changing Climate: Scientists and Kids Explore Global Warming, winner of numerous awards, by Lynne Cherry and Gary Braasch, presenting the changes in flora and fauna and other natural indicators behind climate change. Teacher's guide available.

THE UNIVERSE SERIES: a science-based history of the universe, compellingly told by the universe as an "autobiography," by Jennifer Morgan, illustrated by Dana Lynne Andersen:

Born with a Bang: The Universe Tells Our Cosmic Story;
From Lava to Life: The Universe Tells Our Earth Story; and
Mammals Who Morph: The Universe Tells Our Evolution Story.

Dawn Publications is dedicated to inspiring in children a deeper understanding and appreciation for all life on Earth. To review our titles or to order, please visit us at www.dawnpub.com, or call 800-545-7475.

These are true ocean champions. They used their science to better understand the ocean, and their passion and communications skills to connect people to the ocean and its living creatures and to fight to protect them. — *Jerry R. Schubel, President, Aquarium of the Pacific at Long Beach, California*

We are born with an 'explorer's gene' and children are natural explorers. A lucky few of us have remained enriched by our lifelong curiosity about the ocean. Ocean awareness is, for us, not just a term but a way of life. In this book you will meet ocean people doing what they love best. I hope it inspires many young people to find their own paths to the sea. — *Capt. Don Walsh (USN), PhD, Trieste pilot and Honorary President, The Explorers Club*

Earth Heroes is a wonderful book that reminds us how all the great explorers got their start—with curiosity, intelligence, and a spirit of adventure. — *Wyland, artist/environmentalist*

Every child has the essential tools of a scientist—an insatiable curiosity fueled by observing the world around them, an endless stream of questions based on those observations, and myriad ideas—right and wrong—about the answers. This extraordinary book tells the personal stories of eight remarkable individuals who never lost their curiosity about the mysteries of the ocean, which when combined with lots of hard work allowed them to make tremendous contributions to the exploration, understanding, and protection of Earth's ocean. — *Dr. R. Max Holmes, Woods Hole Research Center scientist*

Dr. Genie Clark, the "Shark Lady," was our Founding Director, and Dr. Sylvia Earle, "Her Deepness," was also at one time a Mote Director. Both began their long careers as curious young explorers, and became forerunners in marine science. It will please them to know that young people who read their stories will be inspired to keep learning and caring for our great oceans, perhaps becoming "champions" themselves. — *Kumar Mahadevan, PhD, President, Mote Marine Laboratory*